James A. Michener

LITERATURE AND LIFE SERIES
(Formerly Modern Literature and World Dramatists)
GENERAL EDITOR: PHILIP WINSOR

Selected list of titles:

SHERWOOD ANDERSON *Welford Dunaway Taylor*
JAMES BALDWIN *Carolyn Wedin Sylvander*
SAUL BELLOW *Brigitte Scheer-Schäzler*
ANTHONY BURGESS *Samuel Coale*
TRUMAN CAPOTE *Helen S. Garson*
WILLA CATHER *Dorothy Tuck McFarland*
JOHN CHEEVER *Samuel Coale*
JOSEPH CONRAD *Martin Tucker*
JOAN DIDION *Katherine Usher Henderson*
JOHN DOS PASSOS *George J. Becker*
THEODORE DREISER *James Lundquist*
T. S. ELIOT *Burton Raffel*
WILLIAM FAULKNER *Joachim Seyppel*
F. SCOTT FITZGERALD *Rose Adrienne Gallo*
FORD MADOX FORD *Sondra J. Stang*
JOHN FOWLES *Barry N. Olshen*
ROBERT FROST *Elaine Barry*
ELLEN GLASGOW *Marcelle Thiébaux*
ROBERT GRAVES *Katherine Snipes*
ERNEST HEMINGWAY *Samuel Shaw*
CHESTER HIMES *James Lundquist*
JOHN IRVING *Gabriel Miller*
CHRISTOPHER ISHERWOOD *Claude J. Summers*
SARAH ORNE JEWETT *Josephine Donovan*
JAMES JOYCE *Armin Arnold*
KEN KESEY *Barry H. Leeds*
RING LARDNER *Elizabeth Evans*
D. H. LAWRENCE *George J. Becker*
C. S. LEWIS *Margaret Patterson Hannay*
SINCLAIR LEWIS *James Lundquist*
ROBERT LOWELL *Burton Raffel*
NORMAN MAILER *Phillip H. Bufithis*
BERNARD MALAMUD *Sheldon J. Hershinow*
MARY MCCARTHY *Willene Schaefer Hardy*
CARSON MCCULLERS *Richard M. Cook*

(continued on last page of book)

JAMES A. MICHENER

George J. Becker

FREDERICK UNGAR PUBLISHING CO.
NEW YORK

Library of Congress Cataloging in Publication Data

Becker, George Joseph.
  James A. Michener.

  (Literature and life series)
  Bibliography: p.
  Includes index.
  1. Michener, James A. (James Albert), 1907–
—Criticism and interpretation.   I.Title.   II. Series.
PS3525.I19Z56   1983   813′.54   82-40279
ISBN 0-8044-2044-0

Contents

Chronology

1907   James Albert Michener, a foundling, is born on February 3 and rescued by Mabel Michener of Doylestown, Pennsylvania.

1921–25   Michener attends Doylestown High School, where he is a member of a champion basketball team.

1925–29   Admitted to Swarthmore College on an Open Scholarship, Michener is enrolled in the Honors program and is graduated with Highest Honors. He becomes a member of the Society of Friends while in college.

1929–31   Michener teaches at The Hill School in Pottstown, Pennsylvania.

1931–33   The recipient of a Joshua Lippincott fellowship, Michener travels and studies abroad, visiting Spain for the first time.

1933–36   Michener teaches English at George School, a Quaker institution in Bucks County.

1936–39   Michener is an associate professor at the Colorado State College of Education at Greeley, from which he receives an M.A. degree in 1937.

1939–40	Michener is a visiting lecturer in the Graduate School of Education at Harvard University.
1940–49	Michener is a social studies editor with the Macmillan Publishing Company in New York City.
1943–46	Having enlisted in the Naval Reserve, Michener is activated in 1943, is posted to the South Pacific in the spring of 1944; he leaves the service with the rank of lieutenant commander.
1947	*Tales of the South Pacific* published.
1948	A Pulitzer Prize is awarded Michener.
1949	The Rodgers and Hammerstein musical *South Pacific* opens in New York and runs for 1,925 performances.
1950	After the Korean war breaks out, Michener visits Japan for the first time.
1953	Michener becomes president of the Asia Institute.
1954	*The Floating World* published. Michener receives an honorary degree of Doctor of Humane Letters from Swarthmore College.
1955	Michener is married to Mari Yoriko Sabusawa, his third marriage.
1956	On his return from a reportorial journey in Asia, Michener is on hand during the Hungarian revolt and rushes his account of it, *The Bridge at Andau,* into print early in the next year.
1959	The Micheners place their collection of Japanese prints in the Honolulu Academy of Arts, which will eventually have title to the entire collection. *Hawaii,* the first of his "blockbuster" novels, published.
1960	Michener is appointed chairman of the Bucks County Citizens for Kennedy, and campaigns actively.
1962	Michener, as a Democrat, runs unsuccessfully for Congress from the Eighth Congressional District in Pennsylvania.
1965	*The Source* published.

1967–68	Michener is secretary of the Pennsylvania Constitutional Convention and head of the Pennsylvania electors. *Iberia* published. The Michener Collection of Contemporary American Painting is received by the University of Texas at Austin.
1970–74	Michener serves as a member of the United States Advisory Commission on Information.
1972	With President Nixon, Michener visits China and Russia as a correspondent.
1974	*Centennial* published.
1977	Michener receives the Medal of Freedom. He begins a series of television programs entitled "The World of James A. Michener."
1978	*Chesapeake* published. Michener receives the Pennsylvania Society Gold Medal.
1979–present	Michener serves on the NASA Advisory Council.
1980	*The Covenant* published. Michener receives the Franklin Award and the Spanish Institute Gold medal. He is a member of the Afghanistan Relief Committee.
1982	*Space* published.

1

A Traveler in Realms of Gold

If it is said of D. H. Lawrence that he is not a classic but an experience, then it is fitting to say of James A. Michener that he is not a classic but a phenomenon—a phenomenon of magnitude.

Michener is undoubtedly the most widely known of this country's serious contemporary novelists, and the most widely read. While the name of no American novelist since Mark Twain can be said to be a household word, recognition of the name of Michener is widespread—not to mention recognition of his face through the dissemination of some dozen television programs in which he has been the narrator and of the occasional television commercial in which he figures. His multifarious writings have brought in a torrent of royalties, again not equaled by any other serious novelist. A few years ago Michener wryly calculated that his writings and the artistic products derived from them—for example, various movies and the musical comedy *South Pacific*—had generated something like seventy million dollars in income tax revenue for the federal government. What is more impressive, however, is the millions of dollars that he and his wife have contributed directly (and deferredly by testament) to education and the arts.

It is characteristic of Michener that while he eagerly encourages the cultivation of his public image, he is reticent about the private man. Generous in permitting

1

interviews in depth, he manages to give a minimum of information about his inner being. He asserts that he will never write an autobiography, leaving it to biographers to plumb his depths as they will. In fact, there are two biographies of Michener in progress. One, by John Kings, commissioned as a seventy-fifth-birthday present, has not yet appeared. The other, by John P. Hayes, will be offered this year to the English department of Temple University as a Ph.D. dissertation.

The origins of James Albert Michener are obscure. The official story is that he was a foundling, born in New York City (or alternatively Doylestown, Pennsylvania) on February 3, 1907, and rescued by Mabel Michener, a widow living in Doylestown. He says he was not aware of his putative bastardy until he was in his teens. There was a momentary emotional disorientation as a result of this revelation, which he quickly overcame. He is willing to admit that awareness of his uncertain antecedents may be a factor in his compulsion to make his mark in the world, but he believes that childhood poverty must have been a factor of at least equal force.

The poverty was extreme. Mabel Michener, who provided foster homes for some thirteen boys in all, took in washing and did sewing at sweatshop wages. Finishing buttonholes was her specialty. Young Jim learned very early to take the interurban into Philadelphia to deliver his mother's work. He worked to supplement the meager income in any way that he could and acquired a basic belief in and admiration for hard work. Even so, on two occasions he lived for a period in the county poorhouse. Long before the Depression, therefore, Michener was aware of the insecurities and indignities of poverty. Even today, he says, he acts on the assumption that his wealth and ease could suddenly be swept away.

Jim Michener entered Doylestown High School in

the fall of 1921 after a summer of hitchhiking that took him to forty-five states, during which he discovered that people were remarkably friendly and hospitable, at least to the young, and developed a passion for travel and a conviction that he could make his way almost anywhere. He did not get to travel again for ten years, but after graduation from college, travel became a major dimension of his life.

One of his high school teachers, Hanna Kirk Mathews, says of him that:

Jim was bright, never worked very hard—he didn't need to in that environment. He wrote rather better than a lot in his class, but I never would have guessed that he would become a successful writer.

She remembers him chiefly as a helpful, friendly boy with a sense of humor. To Michener himself the basic memory of high school is his participation in athletics, which, he says in *Sports in America* and elsewhere, saved him from becoming a pool-hall lout or a streetcorner loafer. He was a player on a champion high school basketball team, received proud recognition from townspeople, and developed a sense of usefulness and importance in his world. As late as 1976 (in *Sports in America*) he was saying that he went to Swarthmore College on an athletic scholarship. This is demonstrably untrue, but no doubt the young man's basketball fame was a factor in his being awarded one of the first Swarthmore Open Scholarships. Ironically, he did not "make it" on the Swarthmore basketball team. He did edit *The Phoenix*, the college weekly newspaper, and he acted in college plays.

In later years Michener has been somewhat ambivalent about the value of a college education, even at Swarthmore, but he is quick to acknowledge that he did benefit from those years. He was accepted into the Honors program, a unique innovation in American education by which in his last two years he took eight seminars, two each semester, and was examined by outside examiners.[1] Michener took four seminars in English literature, two in history, and two in philosophy. He was the first English major to be graduated with Highest Honors, the Swarthmore designation of the more common *summa cum laude*. A favorite story about Michener is that in an oral examination, Conyers Read, a visiting examiner in history, asked a question to which the young man responded eagerly and at length. When he finally had to pause for breath, the examiner broke in with "Very interesting, Mr. Michener, and completely wrong." Michener looks upon the Honors experience as one in which he learned how to learn. As an author, he says, he gives himself "a seminar in advanced studies" as he prepares to write a book. This accurately reflects his total concentration on—immersion in, even—a new subject, aided by temporary total recall of the materials related to the project. Writing weekly seminar papers at Swarthmore may well have provided the foundation for that power.

Since Michener today has little to say about his early years, the best, though highly ambiguous, testimony is to be found in his second novel, *The Fires of Spring*, published in 1949. This novel is no worse—is perhaps even better—than the run of semi-autobiographical novels about growing up to which American novelists are particularly addicted. It does to a very limited extent depict identifiable situations in Michener's life. It also indulges in extravagantly sensational episodes in which adolescent wishful thinking goes far beyond experience—though one must concede that wishful thinking is a part of adolescent groping for meaning and value. In fact, if the reader decides early on that there is a paucity of literal life story in this novel, he is then able to speculate as to how much it tells obliquely about

Michener's unique struggle for identity and maturity in the person of his protagonist, David Harper.

Young Harper lives, in fact, in the poorhouse, where his stubbornly limited Aunt Reba has a job. He is not quite eleven when he learns by hearing the *Iliad* read in school that the "good guys" often lose, like Hector. And, from observing the inhabitants of the poorhouse, Harper is forced to conclude that well-meaning and gentle people often lose in real life. More important is the way young David rises above circumstance, taking refuge in the increasingly secure citadel of himself. He becomes aware of painting through a magazine print of one of Rembrandt's canvases, of music at a Sousa concert at Paradise (Willow Grove amusement park, north of Philadelphia). From old Daniel, dying of cancer, he hears of the joys of money and travel. We see nascent values emerge even out of the deprivations of youth.

The second section of the book, "Paradise," is revealing only in its florid adolescent daydream of sex and minor criminality, going, we trust, far beyond anything Michener experienced when he worked at Willow Grove. The novel presents a continual contrast between the murky morals of Paradise and the cleanness of sport, as David inhabits "multiple schizophrenic worlds."

"Fair Dedham," a part of the novel which relates David's experiences in a Quaker college, bears some resemblance to Michener's experiences. The college is recognizably Swarthmore, even though the novel provides that college with a separate existence as Dedham's rival. To cite only two recognizable details, there are the vision of the local train (the Media local), as it rounds the bend coming into the college station, and the existence of an exclusive girls' school on the edge of town (Mary Lyon School, which became a Navy convalescence hospital during World War II and has since then been used as dormitories by Swarthmore College). The most important correspondence is that of the Readings program at Dedham, an accurate facsimile of the Swarthmore Honors program.

Major personalities and events, however, are not attachable to real persons and occurrences, are, in fact, hyperbolic and sensational. What is important in this section is a general assessment, to a large extent unfavorable, of American higher education in the late 1920s. David finds, or is led to find by the iconoclastic Doc Chisholm out of Texas, that American colleges are outposts of English culture, their sapless object of professorial veneration. (David does not discover until later how barren England was in music and art, because the Quaker college had little interest in those sensuous accomplishments.) In general, there is a "shameless sycophancy," a snobbish condescension toward things American; interest in American culture is nonexistent and American literature is not taught.[2]

David becomes aware at this time, as Michener did then or later, that significant literary culture must go far beyond the hallowed and sterile classroom classics. This was essentially the position taken by the editors of the Modern Library editions beginning in 1912: that it was necessary to become acquainted with French and Russian and Danish and Dutch writers, who dealt honestly and unflinchingly with the modern world. Doc Chisholm's message is that since the United States is destined for leadership in the twentieth century, "We got to have a knowledge worthy of that leadership." And it was to modern prose fiction, primarily, that both David Harper and James Michener turned.

It is significant that *The Fires of Spring*, published in 1949, makes no use of the actual materials of Michener's life from 1929 on, a period of nearly two decades. When he graduated from Swarthmore, the world may have lain

all before him, his to choose, but in fact it took him
nearly twenty years to find his vocation. In the meantime
he tried his hand at teaching in high school and in college, at being a social studies editor for Macmillan, and
at being a junior naval officer and naval historian. Again
it must be emphasized how little Michener has told about
his personal life, about the ups and downs of personal
feeling during the uncertain years of Depression and
war, before success suddenly overtook him.

Michener taught at The Hill School in Pottstown,
Pennsylvania, for two years. Then, having taken time
out to travel and study abroad on a Lippincott fellowship
from Swarthmore, he taught English for three years at
George School, a distinguished Quaker institution in
Bucks County. In 1936 he went to Colorado State College of Education at Greeley to teach and to work for
a master of arts degree. His academic career concluded
with a visiting lectureship at the Harvard Graduate School
of Education in 1939–40. During these years of teaching, Michener began to make a name for himself in the
world of education, publishing some fifteen articles from
1936 to 1942. It is easy to project that from this energetic
beginning he might easily have become highly successful, ending up in a major graduate school with occasional
forays into state and federal educational bureaucracies.

Fortunately for his own self-esteem as well as for
literature, Michener escaped that net. In 1940 he became
a social science editor for Macmillan in New York—
chosen, he says, because his age and interests were right
for a spot in that publisher's table of organization. Again
he was saved from a possibly dull, if respectable, career
in the flourishing world of textbook publishing, first by
the outbreak of war with Japan and, after his return to
civilian life, by a share in the royalties from *South Pacific*.
He left Macmillan in 1949, never to hold a job thereafter.
He was finally, at the age of forty-two, able to pursue

his own course without the constrictions of a nine-to-
five timetable and a hierarchical organization. He was,
as nearly as it is possible to be, a free man.

That freedom and change of direction had come for
Michener as they did for countless others primarily from
the dislocations of war, which may cause an individual
both to sink into temporary nonentity and at the same
time to discover new horizons, new capacities. Michener
was nearly thirty-five when the war broke out. It was
extremely unlikely that he would be drafted, but he felt
a need to participate in the great crusade of World War
II. He enlisted in the Naval Reserve in October 1942,
was activated as a lieutenant, junior grade, on February
3, 1943, and after nearly a year of desk duty in Washington and Philadelphia was sent to the South Pacific
theater, arriving in Espiritu Santo on April 21, 1944. He
was an aviation inspector of sorts, as well as a publications officer, and toured widely among the islands.
During off-duty hours he wrote *Tales of the South Pacific*.
In mid-1945 Michener was assigned to special duties for
a congressional committee and then to responsibility for
histories of various naval operations in the South Pacific.
He was promoted to lieutenant commander in November 1945 and came back to the United States at the end
of the year, returning to his position with the Macmillan
company.

Financial liberation came from two sources. First
and most important, just before the Broadway musical
South Pacific opened, Richard Rodgers and Oscar Hammerstein III generously and cannily offered Michener a
one-percent participation in that lucrative venture. When
he replied that he had no money, they advanced him
$7,500 to be repaid out of royalties. The musical comedy
ran for 1,925 performances in New York. It has since
had long runs in other major cities; it has been almost
continuously on tour; movie rights and royalties have
been a bonanza. In other words, even though Michener's

share was minuscule, he was guaranteed a basic income that made him independent from that point on. The other source of independence came from the DeWitt Wallaces, publishers of *Reader's Digest*. They wanted to make Michener a staff member, to be sent out on regular assignment. He wisely refused, feeling that such a position would take too much time from what he wanted to do. Instead an arrangement was reached by which virtually anything he submitted would be published, after being edited to the *Digest*'s specifications. Not only has this arrangement provided substantial income over the years, but it early made Michener known to the millions of readers of that publication.

In the 1950s *Reader's Digest* had such regular contributors as Paul de Kruif, Fulton Oursler, Morris L. Ernst, Max Eastman, and Donald Culross Peattie. Michener was initially an adornment of less luster but still a catch. For a decade or more readers could count on finding something of his in the *Digest* every few months. In June 1950 his contributions were inaugurated with "The Milk Run" from *Tales of the South Pacific*. A year later there was "Guadalcanal Today" from *Return to Paradise*. It became customary for the *Digest* to offer Michener's books in abbreviated form more or less concurrently with their regular publication. This was still true in the fall of 1980, when *The Covenant* appeared.

At the time his financial independence was achieved Michener still had personal domestic uncertainty. A first marriage, contracted in 1935, had come to an end after five years of separation during the war. A second marriage lasted seven years and ended less amicably. In the property settlement Michener retained the home he had built at Pipersville in Bucks County, a seventy-acre property where from the beginning he sought to preserve ecological balance. In 1954, while he was doing research on mixed marriages, he met Mari Yoriko Sabusawa, a Nisei who had been sent with her family to

Japanese detention camps at the outbreak of World War
II. They were married in 1955. A woman of education
and professional competence, she has also known how
to stay in the background, providing the order and tran-
quility without which Michener could not have written
or done so much. It is since this marriage that his great
and continuous achievement has taken place.

Michener is right when he remarks that for a major
novelist he got off to an unusually late start. *Tales of the
South Pacific* was published when he was forty, and his
reputation was by no means firmly established by that
book. There are many, indeed, who insist that his receiving the Pulitzer Prize in 1948 was a fluke. Certainly
for the next twelve years, though he published prodi-
giously, Michener gained little if any ground in his assault on the citadel of success. *The Fires of Spring* (1949)
found a steady public but did not add to his reputation.
The two succeeding novels, *The Bridges at Toko-ri* (1953)
and *Sayonara* (1954), used popular subjects but exhibited
little depth of insight. The first of these, a novel about
heroism in war, demonstrates Michener's ability to apply the formulas of streamlined popular fiction. Having
demonstrated his mastery, he says, he was not tempted
to try that type of novel again. Actually it is very good
of its kind. The three divisions, "Sea", "Land," and
"Air," convey a feeling for the loneliness of a man of
character pitted against a world he never made who dies
shouldering unwelcome responsibility in a war that has
to be fought, as always, at the wrong time in the wrong
place. In his simple outlines, against such a stark background, the protagonist, Harry Brubaker, a navy aviator
who flies to his death in an attack on some key bridges,
is a memorable figure.

During this period, however, Michener made the
most of an aroused American interest in the new world
of the Pacific. Thus it was that he published *Return to
Paradise* (1951), a combination of documentary and short

story in pairs, in which he expanded his previous acquaintance with islands in the South Pacific to include
Australia and New Zealand. *The Voice of Asia*, in the
same year, was a collection of articles that he had done
on assignment for various magazines or had had published in *Reader's Digest*. By 1952 Orville Prescott of the
New York Times, whose enthusiasm over *Tales of the
South Pacific* had launched Michener's fame, was about
ready to write him off as a serious man of letters: "The
evidence is piling up that as Mr. Michener becomes more
expert as a journalist he is becoming less effective as a
writer of fiction." The profession of journalist was, of
course, respectable, "But those who were excited by the
appearance of the wonderful tales cannot help being disappointed."[3]

It was during his journalistic peregrinations that
Michener became acquainted with the primitive and outwardly romantic life of Afghanistan, an enthusiasm that
led him to visit the country on three occasions and which
produced belatedly, in 1963, one of his most delightful
novels, *Caravans*. The plot was a romantic absurdity to
which few readers paid any attention. Instead they were
attracted by a fresh and substantive contrast of two cultures. In an explanatory appendix Michener attested to
the validity of his description set in 1946, but pointed
out that this primitive world had by 1963 changed fun-
damentally. (Or so he thought. The puritanical mullahs
whom he described have more than a superficial resemblance to the clerical cohorts of Ayatollah Khomeini in
Iran in the present decade.) Michener said he remembered Afghanistan as "an exciting, violent, provocative
place." It was "one of the world's great cauldrons." He
appreciated both the wild and chaotic landscape that
tried human endurance and the violent individualism of
the Afghan male, who has refused into the mid-twen-
tieth century to knuckle under to compulsions from
outside his inherited culture.

In addition to his various magazine articles in the mid-1950s Michener, more or less by accident, engaged in an especially important piece of reporting. He was in Europe on his way back from Asia when the Russians clamped down on the Hungarian uprising that began on October 23, 1956. *Reader's Digest* sent him to Vienna to cover what was happening or would happen in Hungary. The outcome was a firsthand account entitled *The Bridge at Andau*, which went to press at the end of January, in 1957. The bridge in question was a rickety wooden affair—not sturdy enough to bear even a motorcycle in motion—which spanned a canal adjacent to the Austro-Hungarian boundary. Perhaps as many as 25,000 Hungarians fled over that bridge. With the connivance of the Austrian border patrol, Michener on several occasions actually went a short distance into Hungary in order to help feeble refugees who could not make it out by themselves.

This book is, among other things, a paean of praise for Austrian generosity and a condemnation of American lack of interest. Michener, who has always been hostile to communism and the communist bloc, asserted that "Hungary rebelled against communism primarily because the young people of the nation wanted intellectual freedom." He saw the revolt, though a failure in the near term, as a turning point in world history: ". . . it is absolutely clear that Russia has lost a propaganda battle of critical proportions." His judgment was much too optimistic. He mistakenly expected other satellite countries to go the same way and gradually to wear down Russian domination. Czechoslovakia, Poland, and Afghanistan are proofs to the contrary. But he was correct that the vision of idyllic well-being under communism entertained by many intellectuals and idealists (Jean-Paul Sartre, for example) had been discredited. The book, though of no analytical importance, was welcome testimony in most of the world. It was translated into fifty-three languages and is the most widely disseminated of Michener's works, though, of course, not the most widely read.

One wonders what Michener thought the future had in store for him when he reached fifty. He was able to live comfortably by working hard at writing and speaking. He had been traveling widely ever since the war. He had indulged in a passionate enthusiasm for Japanese art, and almost ten years before had had the satisfaction of winning a Pulitzer Prize. All this was admirable, but if he was to make a real name for himself he had to find a more impressive medium. He was lucky enough, astute enough, brilliant enough—we may take our choice—to rise to a new level of achievement by means of what reviewers have called his "blockbuster" novels, his "docudramas," his panoramic, and one might add "panchronic," novels, beginning with *Hawaii* in 1959. This novel was followed by four others, of equal magnitude if not equal importance. They will be the major object of examination in chapters that follow, but it should be kept in mind that this achievement, significant as it is, has not satisfied Michener's ambition. Almost immediately after the success of *Hawaii* was manifest, he pursued another goal, that of becoming a public figure either in politics or behind the scenes in government or as a respected media personality.

After participation in the John F. Kennedy campaign in 1960, to which we will return in a moment, Michener decided to run for Congress from the Eighth Congressional District in Pennsylvania (conservative Bucks and Lehigh counties). What success in this endeavor would have done to his writing is easy to estimate. Michener says that he would have expected to serve in Congress for six or seven terms, then to return to his writing. It is more likely that his career as novelist, barely begun, would have been over.

His involvement in politics during the 1960s brought

forth two books. The first, *Report of the County Chairman*
(1961), is pretentiously titled. Michener was not the
elected county chairman of the Democratic party (he
was at that point not even a Democrat), but was chosen
by *the* chairman to be chairman of a special drive to
swing Republican and Independent voters over to Kennedy. Michener felt no particular antagonism toward
Richard Nixon, but he felt strongly that the presidency
and the stature of the United States in the world had
been depreciated by the Eisenhower administration. He
became a Democrat not merely because of hopeful enthusiasm for Kennedy but because of his encounters with
conservatism and bigotry among his Republican audi-
ences. In the last days of the campaign he joined a barn-
storming group covering the Middle West and some of
the Mountain States with such luminaries as Joan and
Ethel Kennedy, Stan Musial of baseball fame, and Ar-
thur Schlesinger, Jr. He says it was the behavior of Republicans in Boise, Idaho, that made him a confirmed
liberal, "totally committed to the liberalism of the cities
rather than to the conservatism of the rural areas," beautiful though they were. In rural Bucks County, even
though leavened by the citydwellers of the new Levit-
town, the voters went for Nixon 67,000 to 57,000. In
fact, every district in which Michener spoke went for
Nixon. But the country chose Kennedy by a narrow
margin, and Michener was glad that "the anti-intellectualism," "the deification of the country club," and "the
conservatism of the last eight years" were over.

   Report of the County Chairman, a pleasantly anecdotal
if somewhat self-glorifying volume, was followed at the
end of the decade by an essentially crusading work,
*Presidential Lottery: The Reckless Gamble in Our Electoral
System* (1969). It began with a personal account of the
1968 election, when Michener was the head of the Pennsylvania electors (Hubert Humphrey carried Pennsyl-

vania). The argument of the book was that both the electoral college and the provision of the Constitution that throws election into the House of Representatives when no candidate has a majority "must be abolished before they wreck our democracy." The argument was sound enough, but a decade and a half after it was presented there is no disposition on the part of the voters at large to avoid the evils that Michener foresaw.

The most significant journalistic, novelistic, and moral concern of Michener's for more or less the last two decades has been the stresses and false values that beset American youth—indeed, the youth in advanced industrial societies generally. He first attacked the problem in a novel, *The Drifters* (1971). This was a depiction of a cross section of six dropouts who have gathered together in Torremolinos, indulge somewhat harmlessly in touristic wanderings to Portugal and to Pamplona in northern Spain (for the bullrunning), but later are engulfed in the decadence of Marrakech and Tangier. The tone of the novel is basically sympathetic, but there is a limit to paternal indulgence, and the conclusion, in addition to bringing the death of one of the group from drug addiction, is not hopeful. The reader must conclude that a substantial number of dissident youth are doomed.

Simultaneously with *The Drifters*, Michener was called upon by *Reader's Digest* to do a documentary on the violent weekend at Kent State University on May 1–4, 1970. This is the chief instance of the author's reliance on a research team, made up both of outsiders and of members of the college community. Michener's wife, a graduate of nearby Antioch College, talked to students and faculty members. Michener, who arrived on campus unheralded in early August, sat in bars and just listened for a week. Then he let it be known that he would be happy to talk with all comers—and they came in droves. His conclusion, after this great mass of information was sifted and correlated, was that "This is as true a picture of one small aspect of a great state university as we could construct."

The account is as free of bias as is humanly possible, certainly more free than the findings of the grand jury called by the state attorney-general, whose aim seemed to be "solely to arrest students and professors who had caused the trouble." Michener's book has not been superseded by later publications. Rather, as student activism has subsided, it has been pushed to one side as of less vital concern than was thought at that time. The book is a human and appealing piece of reporting. It is always clear, and in its account of the events of Friday night and Monday morning it is highly dramatic. No doubt the author was under obligation to proceed from the *what* to the *why*, but the two goals are not entirely compatible under pressure and without a much broader perspective. Michener's judgment was that what happened was essentially an unlucky accident, a combination of student naïveté and National Guard weariness. Of the four victims, two were there by chance, two were guilty of some involvement. But "No student performed any act on May 4 for which he deserved to be shot." However, the book's major conclusion was:

The hard-core revolutionary leadership across the nation was so determined to force a confrontation...that some sort of major incident had become inevitable.

Here as elsewhere Michener showed himself "perpetually concerned about what young people are doing." The individual portraits were generally sympathetic, but the overall impression was one of widespread juvenile irresponsibility. The last section, "The Girl with the Delacroix Face," was by its studied objectivity revealing and utterly damning. The girl whose grief-stricken posture over the body of Jeff Miller was caught on film and reproduced all over the country was in fact a fourteen-year-old runaway from Florida who just happened to be on the Kent State campus that weekend. She had no awareness of what was going on, and afterward she had no clear recollection of what she had experienced. It was an effective ending for this book, though it no doubt offended the dissident young by its demonstration of mental and social irresponsibility.

Sports in America (1976), though a badly organized and a discursive book (much of the research was done by others), had nonetheless a potential for greater impact than any other pieces of Michener's nonfiction writing except perhaps *Iberia*. I say "potential," for American society is so addicted to and so dominated by sports that few may have paused to weigh the charges the book brought. Michener's basic query is: "Should a well-run society divert so high a percentage of its gross national product into sports, when there are so many other aspects of our national life which cry for attention?" A horrendous gap exists between the idyllic mythic world of sports in an earlier America and the sordid facts of sports concealed by a cynical perpetuation of that myth by the media. To cite only a few of the condemnatory theses that Michener nailed to the wall of media complacency: "Black salvation through sport is an enervating myth." "Obsession with sports is destructive to black youth." "Acceptance of a college athletic scholarship may be the first step to a truncated career." "The athlete and his coach move in a world of conservative values and are surrounded by conservative types." And: coaches tend to think that Nixon was persecuted "by the same kind of longhaired radicals who give coaches so much trouble on college faculties."

There was no doubt in Michener's mind about the abiding attraction and value of sports. They could be a moral revelation of the need for and the way to humility. He found "competition to be the rule of nature, tension to be the structure of the universe," but he objected to deliberate exploitation of those needs. Sports could and should be fun. While working with radical youth groups in the 1960s, and in discussions with young people generally, Michener was told over and over again that they were "turned off by the excesses of organized sports, the adults who controlled it and the jocks who participated." There was a "lack of noblesse oblige among the newer crops of athletes." "They become wandering mercenaries, much like the German knights of the late Middle Ages, generating few local loyalties." Yet Michener was all for sports if properly practiced, and he attested to the life-saving role they had played in his own life, first as a boy and later after his heart attacks. His conclusion was very simple:

I want our country to protect, and augment, and make available such experience to others. For it is this enlarging of the human adventure that sports are all about.

Michener's one fictioinal venture into contemporary chronicling of American life concerns another enlarging of the human adventure. In its scope and varied focus his most recent novel, *Space* (1982), makes one think of Dos Passos's *Midcentury* and *Century's Ebb*, though it is not patterned after those works. Michener sets out to chronicle the American space effort from its shadowy beginnings in 1944 to its winding down in 1982. Because of his experience as a member of the NASA Advisory Council he conducts this narrative with assurance and informed competence, not to mention enthusiasm, although even so there are on occasion rather heavy doses of scientific information which the reader must gulp down. This novel is likely, for the short term at least, to be one of the writer's most popular works. Certainly it is an authentic and balanced introduction to the space age, and two of its narrative episodes are intense and memorable, in particular the one that takes place on the previously unexplored dark side of the moon. It should be added that in this novel Michener for the first time provides a considerable amount of rough language, especially from the mouth of Randy Claggett, a Texas astronaut. He also provides a genuinely funny dirty story involving Roosevelt, Stalin, and Churchill at Teheran.

The way the novel opens is particularly effective. We are introduced to four of the leading characters in various parts of the world on October 24, 1944. The first scene is set at a rocket-tracking station thirteen miles south of London, where Stanley Mott, an American engineer, watches a German V-2 rocket coming in at more than 2,000 miles an hour. His concern, however, is with the German installation at Peenemünde on the Baltic coast, where research on atomic weapons is being conducted. With authority from the President he instructs the U.S. Air Force bombing squadron not to hit the living quarters at Peenemünde because it is imperative to capture three of the chief scientists alive. (One of the three is in fact killed.) At the same time, the climactic naval battle of Leyte Gulf is beginning in the Pacific. Norman Grant, a small-town lawyer in peacetime, is captain of a destroyer escort vessel. Unhesitatingly he takes on Japanese battleships, and when his ship is in its turn sunk, he heroically swims in shark-infested waters to allow one of his wounded men (a black) room on the life raft.

On that same day John Pope, a seventeen-year-old in Grant's hometown of Clay in the fictional state of Fremont, has three experiences of great magnitude. He is the member of the high school football team who is chiefly responsible for their defeating their arch-rival. That night for the first time he looks at the heavens through high-powered binoculars and realizes that the stars have reached out and grabbed him—a possession that will never leave him. As he is looking through the binoculars, his girl friend, Penny, with whom he has broken a date, determinedly joins him, and in his euphoria he engages for the first time in rapturous sexual intercourse. The final episode on this day takes the reader to Peenemünde, where Dieter Kolff, one of the scientists whom Stanley Mott must rescue, escapes the bombing because he has gone off base to meet with his girlfriend, Liesl.

As the war ends, Kolff is able to join the Americans, largely through the ingenuity of a Nazi SS officer, who manages to turn defeat to his advantages and in time becomes a power in the American aerospace industry. Wernher von Braun is also grabbed by the Americans, and this real figure is the mainstay of the American rocket and space effort for thirty years. Grant goes home to Fremont a hero, is elected to the U.S. Senate, and, though unimaginative, does come around to supporting the space effort. Mott has a somewhat roving commission to forward the efforts of the various space facilities, a mission that he fulfills with such devoted intensity that he ignores his family; one of his sons becomes a homosexual and the other, a drug runner, is killed. John Pope joins the Navy, gets himself appointed to Annapolis, and becomes a leading astronaut. He is ably seconded by his wife, Penny, who after receiving her law degree works for Senator Grant and Senator Glancey and in time becomes the administrative head of the Congress's space committee. She challenges Grant in 1982 and is elected to the Senate in her turn.

These four figures, and those who are attached to them, are the vertebrae of the space program as the novel anatomizes it. As the novel ends, they have reached a senior status from which they must pass the torch to a younger generation—with this difference: the age of manned exploration and consequent public enthusiasm is over. Hereafter, exploration of the remote reaches of this galaxy and its neighbors must, for the foreseeable future at least, be left to intricate machines. The novel's heroes, and particularly the six fictional astronauts whose careers we follow (John Pope being one of them), are the Titans of the space age. As a journalist, Cynthia Rhee, says of them, they are immortal: they will be read about five hundred years from now "the way we read about Magellan today."

The novel gives an orderly account of the various stages of American space activity and of the disorderly jockeying for position by the armed services, by Congress, and by private industry. Once Kolff, Wernher von Braun, and a hundred other German scientists have been brought to the United States to work on rocketry, they find themselves in an uncertain haven. What is to be done with them and their talents is subject to the opposition of an unimaginative and cost-conscious Congress and Administration. Their potential for space exploration is always there, but it is not until American complacency is jarred by the Sputnik flight in October 1957 that ambitious participation in the space age begins—to a degree for the wrong motive; that is, more out of rivalry with the Russians than in acceptance of the superb challenge of new explorations, new intellectual horizons.

Basic disagreement with America's vision comes from those such as Dieter Kolff, who know that the giant steps for mankind will in fact be of strictly technological nature, that space explorations will of necessity be largely unmanned, and that the sending of astronauts to the moon (a neighboring irrelevance) or generally into orbit is merely a costly publicity gimmick. Members of Congress point out that human interest is the only lever by which to get public support and to pry money out of Congress—an opinion that prevails and is vindicated in the seventies, as public interest diminishes unless it is regenerated by the tremendous publicity for the manned shuttle flights or for the penetration to Mars and Saturn.

The second half of the novel brings to the fore the six astronauts and their wives. These characters are differentiated more by origin and armed service affiliation than by individual traits. Since their lives are highly specialized, they are almost forced into generic roles. Certainly this is true as far as the public-relations officer is concerned: if he had his way they would all conform to a stereotype. The same is true for the wives, who are looked upon as public-relations resources during and after manned space flights, especially in case of the death of an astronaut. Fortunately, we can follow with interest and attention the careers of two of the six men. John Pope and Randy Claggett, who had first met in Korea, are contrasting personalities—one a straight arrow, the other a rambunctious Texan. Their ill-fated expedition to the dark side of the moon is the highpoint of the narrative. Claggett and Dr. Paul Linley, a civilian scientist (and nephew of the black sailor whom Senator Grant saved at Leyte Gulf), are exploring on foot when there is a sudden burst of sunspot activity. Protected only by their space suits, they rush for the landing vehicle but are already so enfeebled by radiation sickness that they are unable to manage a complete takeoff, and fall to their death. Pope, in the orbiting vehicle, risks his life to make sure they are dead before he carries out the unprecedented task of bringing the spacecraft back to earth single-handed.

When their spaceflight careers are over, the men disperse into various activities, like real-life John Glenn to the Senate and Frank Borman to Eastern Airlines. John Pope becomes a professor of astronomy at the university in his hometown. Even though the men have "produced no national spokesman for space, no poet of the skies like Saint-Exupéry of France," their achievement has been beyond measure. Writes Michener:

Man reached the planets. He stood challenging the entire solar system to reveal its secrets. Even the ramparts of the Galaxy were now approachable, and where this vast adventure into space would end, no man could predict.

As Stanley Mott says in a speech:

I am satisfied by all the evidence that reaches me that the mind of man now stands in much the position it stood at the beginning of the Copernican age. Ahead of us lies one of the world's major explosions of knowledge.

Informed and engrossing as the novel is, it would merely be an interesting and timely chronicle were it not for an unexpected added dimension. This is provided by the initially tangential presence in the narrative of Leopold Strabismus ("Wall-eye" one might call him, the only instance of Michener's using a tag name for a character). He is a charlatan of the first water—and of gradually increasing girth—and he ultimately becomes the spokesman and manipulator of anti-intellectualism in America. Strabismus devises a series of lucrative rackets, all with the uplifting initials USA. First, he creates the United Space Association, which plays on fears of UFOs and invading little green men from outer space. He extracts a good deal of money from Senator Grant's wife, who believes everything he says. Eventually the Grants' daughter, Marcia, who believes nothing he says but is responsive to his sexual magnetism, becomes his lover and coadjutor. After Sputnik, he sets up the University of Space and Aviation, which sells degrees. Marcia is the dean of its nonexistent faculty. In the 1970s he is inspired to expand into religion, with the United Salvation Alliance, and becomes a public figure. He plays on the fears and prejudices of the uneducated and the uncritical, using them, he says, because they want to be used.

Although at first his portrait seems to be a merely satirical device, toward the end of the novel we realize that Strabismus's crusade against what he calls "scientific atheism" and "atheistic humanism" by a return to fundamentalist religion is a direct challenge to the new explosion of knowledge. He and his followers picket lectures by national park rangers telling about the geological history of those areas; there is a successful referendum in Fremont forbidding the teaching of biological or geological evolution; there are impassioned attacks against librarians and college professors for their atheistic/communistic indoctrination of the young; and for good measure there are an attack on homosexuals and the beginnings of a virulent anti-Semitism.

What we have is a confrontation, on the level of ideas, between Strabismus and his followers on the one hand and people like Stanley Mott and John Pope on the other. Mott accuses Strabismus of becoming the "Jim Jones of the mind." But Mott also recognizes the fault that lies "in men like himself who had blindly pursued their own defined interests while ignoring the vast, sloppy, stumbling universe of people who could not keep pace with the discoveries." It is in this connection that Mott's study of circadian disorientation, or jet lag, has expanded relevance. One can infer that a blind reaction against new concepts, new discoveries, is a parallel disorientation of the mind and spirit.

What this confrontation boils down to is the age-old diversity of doctrine about the origin, design, and governance of the universe. Mott has, once, in an argument with his minister father, made a concession, an intellectual trade: he would accept the idea that a scientist's conception of a primal force might be called God. In return his father was willing to allow him his billion years for the creative activity of that force. Strabismus will allow no such accommodation. As far as he is concerned, the earth was created in 4004 B.C., and on that day God put those misleading fossils in the rocks. At a conference exploring the possibility of life on other planets, it is pointed out that if the earth had been positioned only slightly nearer to or farther from the sun, life as we know it could not have developed. Strabismus knows that God put the earth at that exact spot for the purpose of creating life. The voice of the narrator, not of Mott, does perhaps bring these opposed positions closer when, ecstatic over the pictures sent back from the ship orbiting Saturn, he exclaims that "inherent in whatever force created that infinite halo [Saturn's rings] was the artistry of a Michelangelo or a Picasso, for it was a work of art..."

The novel *Space* suggests that we may well be in for a bad time, when the fruits of intellect are derided and destroyed; but from the long perspective of history we are reminded that disputes such as this one had gone on in Assyria and Stonehenge, at Karnak and Machu Picchu... and "a thousand years from now they would still be debated on some planet orbiting some other star in some other galaxy."

Two secondary and nonliterary areas of endeavor have brought the Michener image before the eyes of millions. He has served on a number of government committees, including the United States Advisory Commission on Information from 1970 to 1974, during that time visiting American information service establishments in forty-seven countries. In 1972 he was a presidential cultural envoy to Romania. In 1975 he served as President Gerald Ford's personal ambassador to cultural celebrations in Japan. (He was also a member of the Bicentennial Advisory Committee in this country.) Naturally he was sent to represent the United States at national celebrations in Australia and New Zealand in 1976, and to the independence celebration in the New Hebrides islands in 1980.

In the last five or six years it is the Michener television programs that have widened public awareness of this author. The first of these shows, collectively entitled "The World of James A. Michener," were travelogues showing the countries he had earlier written about: Israel, Hawaii, the South Pacific, and Spain. To these

Poland was added in 1980. The three-part "Sports in America" program, also in 1980, had a hostile reception in some quarters; the reviewer for *Sports Illustrated* found the series boring and told Michener to go back to writing novels.[4]

In 1981 four additional programs (two of them in five parts) were completed and will be syndicated for commercial television showings. These programs have been made and copyrighted by Emlen House Productions in Philadelphia for the purpose of providing Michener "added dimensions in communications, sound and sight, thereby giving people an additional opportunity to communicate with Mr. Michener's greatness," according to a representative of the foundation. The programs have been initiated and supported by Edward Piszek of Philadelphia, a close friend of Michener and an ardent apologist for Poland. It is not surprising, therefore, that the most recent of these television projects include "Poland: The Will to Be," "The Enduring Tradition (Polish Culture)" in five parts, and "John Paul II: The Pope from Poland." It was through Piszek that Michener became acquainted with John Paul II before he became pope. Michener has twice visited him at the Vatican. When the Pope touched down in Anchorage, Alaska, on his way home from the Orient, he is reported to have looked over the group assembled to meet him and to have inquired, "Why didn't they send Michener?"

Michener has said that he probably has two more big books in him. One of them will certainly be a novel about Texas. He made such a promise in a speech to the Texas legislature in the fall of 1981 and has now moved temporarily to Austin to do his research. He is noncommittal about which of the other lively subjects clamoring for his attention will actually be selected. A short, powerful novel on Poland, is reported to be in existence, but no date has been set for publication. Michener and his public will always regret the volumes he didn't write or didn't complete. Michener is evasive regarding the whereabouts of a book on Mexico, which, he says, Random House is eager to publish even in its not quite completed state.

There has been every reason why a man of Michener's talents and background should want to branch out in many directions, should seek to be seer and prophet on contemporary problems, should wish to have an active part in shaping public policy. But the fact remains that if a writer is to have lasting impact, it is most likely to come through his creative works. It is safe to say that four or five decades from now the Michener of the carefully cultivated public image will be largely forgotten, but a winnowed group of his works, including *Iberia* and perhaps *Tales of the South Pacific* as well as the so-called "blockbuster novels," will still be read.

2

Island Worlds of the Pacific

During World War II Michener served on or visited forty-nine Pacific islands, all the way from Iwo Jima (near Japan) to remote Pitcairn Island of *Mutiny on the Bounty* fame. In a *Reader's Digest* article more than thirty years later he confessed to being "a nesomaniac"; that is, one who is crazy about islands.[1] We could also call him a "polynesian," a man from many islands. This love for and rapturous acquaintance with islands he traces back to 1931, when he visited the Outer Hebrides off the coast of Scotland. When he came to the islands of the South Pacific, it was their spiritual force that reinvigorated him. The lure of islands, he says, is that they exist close to nature, that they are small enough to be comprehended, and that each develops in its own way. They also attract eccentrics, who are not always delightful, for the South Sea islands are somewhat uninhibited.

More to the point is the fact that the islands of the Pacific were a revelation to the multitudes who served there during the Second World War, a revelation of other ways of feeling and behaving. Certainly that is what Michener experienced. His most substantial and enduring writing for fifteen years after the war dealt with the islands of the South Pacific, with Japan and its art, and with Hawaii, the perfect melting pot that would produce, he hoped, "the Golden Men."

Tales of the South Pacific

Nowadays, some thirty-five years after an almost dual birth, *Tales of the South Pacific* must be distinguished from the musical comedy of enduring fame. Rodgers and Hammerstein utilized only two sections of Michener's book, sections that are romantic and exotic and largely removed from the experience of war. If the novel makes use of the romantic dreams that lure men to lotus islands, the musical comedy *South Pacific* tops it in hearts.

Michener calls his book a novel, even though in fact it is made up of nineteen casually related episodes, sketches reminiscent in a general way of Turgenev's A *Sportsman's Sketches*. Yet perhaps it is a novel. It does have a coherence that is not initially apparent. The individual episodes do converge to make a whole that is distinctly more than the sum of its parts. The result, if not a war novel, is a novel about men at war in the Pacific during the crucial months of 1942–43, when victory or defeat was hanging in the balance. It is an intensely patriotic novel; it is one that celebrates heroism, though both patriotism and heroism are played down, understated. It is not a blood-and-guts novel, nor one that demonstrates the dehumanization imposed by the military machine, nor one that capitalizes on the absurdities of war in the manner of Joseph Heller's *Catch-22*. There is nothing just like it about World War II. In its uniqueness it is permanent testimony of what that war was like in a major theater of its action.

There are, of course, obstacles in the way of the work's enduring fame. For most people the war in the Pacific has never been as graphic or as specifically locatable as European wars. To be sure, for those of us who on the sidelines, participated in the Pacific war poring over maps, seeking to know exactly where action was taking place, *Tales of the South Pacific* is set on somewhat familiar ground. But for the majority of readers today the setting is merely a vague, watery, empty space on the map, accessible by swift tourist jaunts to international hotels but scarcely having a life or character of its own. Nonetheless, for those who wish to see, it is still an experience of a whole new world of values and behavior, just as it was for the hordes of soldiers, sailors, marines, aviators, and SeaBees in their late teens and early twenties whose eyes were opened, who were intrigued or shocked by the human landscape of the South Pacific. American provincialism encountered human beings of different hue with culture patterns of different texture, and during long periods of inaction waiting for action men at war pondered what the experience meant. The novel states emphatically that theirs was an important experience, that the men who fought in the South Pacific will live a long time in memory, that

They had an American quality. They, like their victories, will be remembered as long as our generation lives. After that, like the men of the Confederacy, they will become strangers. Longer and longer shadows will obscure them, until their Guadalcanal sounds distant on the air like Shiloh and Valley Forge.

It is no qualification of heroism that the novel gives an initial warning that all a man did in the Pacific theater was "sit on his ass and wait."

You rotted on New Caledonia waiting for Guadalcanal. Then you sweated twenty pounds away on Guadal waiting for Bougainville. There were battles, of course. But they were flaming things of the bitter moment. A blinding flash at Tulagi. A day of horror at Tarawa. An evening of terror on Kuralei. Then you relaxed and waited. And pretty soon you hated the man next to you, and you dreaded the look of a coconut tree.

This situation comes into magnified focus as the narrative develops. Significantly, although the battle on Guadalcanal is going on during the early part of the novel, it is not the center of attention. That is reserved for a later (fictional) assault on Kuralei in an action called

"Alligator"—an instance of the tactic called "island hopping," an audacious leaping over Japanese strongholds, which are left to wither on the vine. Once the airstrip is built on Konora it is obvious to the enemy that the American forces are mounting an attack for somewhere. In this case, because of a Japanese officer whose imagination had been sharpened at Cal Tech, resistance on Kuralei is highly effective. Taking the island costs a high price, but the island is taken, and American forces in 1943 are poised to go on to Leyte Gulf, to Okinawa, and ultimately to Japan.

The major action at Kuralei is prepared for early on by mention of the Battle of the Coral Sea, by the preparation of lonely Norfolk Island as a stopping place for planes coming north from New Zealand, and by the episode telling of the heroic English planter, "the Remittance Man," who coolly reports from behind Japanese lines about air and sea activity in "the slot," the sea passage leading to Guadalcanal. The pattern of military action over a vast area of sea and islands emerges gradually. Kuralei is mentioned as early as page 10, but we are a third of the way through the novel before we know what is involved. The characters in the story are themselves in the dark as to where the attack will take place. Thus the emphasis falls on the massive logistic arrangements necessary for an undefined attack and on the human agents of that preparation. The narrator, for example, belongs to LARU 8, that is, Landbased Aircraft Repair Unit 8, which is blown up precisely when it is most needed during the attack on Kuralei. That is war, mostly waiting, mostly preparing for those few agonizing moments when men die suddenly but the wave of men rolls on.

The 1942 decision to go ahead with "Alligator," Michener writes, "changed lives in every country in the world. It exacted a cost from every family in Japan and America." Only the narrator, who flies from Honolulu to Noumea with secret plans for distribution to military outposts, has any knowledge of what is entailed. As he says, "Each of the remaining bits of gossip in this book took place after the participants were committed to Kuralei" without knowing precisely what was involved. He says also:

Alligator was a triumph of mind, first, and then of muscle. It was a rousing victory of the spirit, consummated in the flesh. It was to me . . . a lasting proof that democratic men will ever be the equals of those who deride the system.

"The Airstrip at Konora" provides an instance of the heroic improvisatory action in this preparatory period. The need is to build an airstrip rapidly so that the Japanese will not have time to mobilize an effective attack upon it. There are two major decisions to be made. One is the preferred direction of the strip: Is there a ravine in the way? The second question is whether the coastal mounds of the island contain enough coral to fill that ravine if it exists. Former residents and some military personnel are the first heroes, as they infiltrate behind the Japanese lines to get answers to these questions. The second batch of heroes are the ingenious, zealous SeaBees, who let nothing stop their enterprise as they build the airstrip from both ends while another group frenziedly bulldozes coral into the ravine. The two jobs end simultaneously and on schedule as the first American bombers come sweeping in.

The first-person narrator/observer of this novel is deliberately a somewhat undefined personality. He is only "a paper-work sailor," sent on all sorts of errands, participating on the sidelines in some significant actions, and often, when off duty, going along for the ride to some strange adventures, but never allowing his personality to intrude. In a couple of tales he fades out and Michener uses a strict third-person omniscient stance. In a couple of others a major character takes over without the mediation of the basic narrator. Over all, this is a novel in which Michener has his narrative stance under control—a control that he sometimes lost when he attempted bigger works.

It would be wrong to think of any one character as *the* protagonist, for this is essentially a sampling of men at war fairly carefully distributed among the services. The man who gets the most exposure is a navy lieutenant, Tony Fry. He first appears in the second narrative, entitled "Mutiny," where he shows himself to be sensitive, unconventional, a law unto himself. He is sent to Norfolk Island to resolve the impasse over locating an airstrip in a living cathedral of pines, "the loveliest monument in the South Pacific." He recognizes that the strip must be built but he is also considerate of the feelings of the *Bounty* descendants, and so maneuvers that the admiral makes the decision, thus directing the anger of the islanders at remote authority. In fact, a bulldozer is blown up with Fry's connivance, a kind of moral concession, for, thinking of the Jews at Dachau, he does not like the idea of anybody being mauled.

"The Cave," a long thirty-page episode, shows Fry in greater depth. He is landed on Tulagi to install a radio receiver in a cave in order to receive reports from the Remittance Man. In a way Fry takes over authority from the actual commander of the PT squadron that is stationed at Tulagi. The officers and enlisted men seek him out for his blitheness of spirit and inexhaustible supply of whiskey. They begin to share Tony's speculations about how men can have such courage. The narrator concludes that each man has a cave somewhere, a hidden and sustaining refuge from war, be it love of family, dreams of a new life after the war, even whiskey and desperation, or a kind of incandescent heroism beyond the call of valor. The ending of this narrative is extraordinary. The narrator and the PT commander go along with Fry to rescue the Remittance Man when his broadcasts stop. A native, suffering from elephantiasis, who conveys his gigantic scrotum in a kind of cart, points to the Englishman's head among a row of skulls left by the Japanese. Tony's understanding and compassion can encompass the suffering of both the dead and the living, and he promises to send help to the hapless, courageous native.

Fry's curiosity leads him to contemplate a barbaric native religious rite in "The Boar's Tooth." He goes on a crazy hegira by air with Bus Adams in search of whiskey with which to celebrate Christmas at Segi Point. He is consumed with passion for Latouche Barzan, one of De Becque's daughters (De Becque was played by Ezio Pinza in *South Pacific*), connives at her killing of her hated husband, and marries her, duly putting his affairs in order to her advantage before he goes off to the climactic attack on Kuralei. There his curiosity, or courage, leads to his death. The novel makes no attempt to pass judgment on him. The narrator's grief is without condemnation. Good men blossom in war, and some are killed. There is nothing to be done about it but go on.

A counter-exhibit, one of base metal, is Bill Harbison, a navy officer who in appearance and superficial manner would seem to qualify as the all-American man. He is a Princeton product. (Bryn Mawr women and Princeton men are likely to be pilloried in Michener novels.) He expects his outstanding abilities to be immediately recognized and rewarded by his superiors, and he is disgruntled when he is posted to New Caledonia as recreation officer at Efate, not even to the capital of the island. His duties demand less than an hour's attention a day. He feels that officers and men alike are beneath his notice. Finally he finds solace in sports, especially in volleyball, at which he is very good and by which he gains ungrudging admiration from the men around him. Life brightens even more when a contingent of navy nurses arrives. He outdoes himself being helpful. He gives a barbecue for them. For a time he takes out Dinah Culbert, age forty-two, clearly no threat to his loyalty to his wife. When his attention turns to Nellie Forbush (of *South Pacific* fame), that is a different story. Expecting an easy conquest, he nearly rapes her in frustration, reinstates himself with insincere apology, and causes her to fall in love with him. She is forced to ask him if he intends to marry her—a dash of cold water to his lustful intentions which he transmutes into disdain for a pushy person from provincial Arkansas. Harbison turns up occasionally in later episodes, especially in "Those Who Fraternize," where he shows himself to be a bounder. When the chips are down and the invasion of Kuralei is imminent, this officer, who has long been chafing for action, suddenly uses pull to get himself posted back to the United States. He has no desire to lodge in the cemetery at Hoga Point, and the narrator, grieving for dead Tony Fry, realizes that the absent Harbison is a man whom he can willingly forget.

Bus Adams is another major character, appearing in five episodes, often with Tony Fry. He is the embodiment of the happy-go-lucky, daredevil type of flyer, disdainful of discipline, driving his superiors crazy, but the kind of man by whom wars are won. It is his voice we hear in "A Boar's Tooth" and "Those Who Fraternize," a voice that lends authenticity to this account of men at war.

The two episodes on which Rodgers and Hammerstein drew for *South Pacific* are of very unequal value. "Our Heroine," with Nellie Forbush as central figure, recounts her mixed reaction to Emile De Becque, a planter who fled from France after killing a man and who has fathered eight illegitimate daughters by women of various hues. Aside from the stereotyped love story— in this case one in which Nellie finally accepts the tarnished virtue of her suitor—the narrative makes a point

of the race prejudice this girl from Arkansas has to overcome. She does not so much mind De Becque's indulgence in polygamous affairs as she does the fact that his
Polynesian consort, being black, is a "nigger." It is to
her credit that she overcomes this aversion and in the
story, as in the musical comedy, sings in sweet harmony
with the enchanting, though dusky-hued, maidens she
will have as stepdaughters.

"Fo' Dolla'," on the other hand, is for many readers
the high point of the novel, evoking as it does a vision
of paradise in the fictional island of Bali-ha'i. It is an
account of the love affair between Lieutenant Joe Cable
and Liat, a beautiful island maiden, schooled by French
nuns. Bloody Mary, her mother—a tough, bawdy,
practical Tonkinese trader—has no hesitation about putting her virgin daughter in Joe's way. Love is immediate
and deep, but of necessity brief. Joe, seeking permission
to marry Liat, is ready to give up his stateside ties and
future. Permission is denied. The army moves on to
prepare for the attack on Kuralei. Bloody Mary falls
back on her reserve plan: marriage of her daughter to
an unsavory French planter. Each of the lovers goes on
to an uncertain and diminished future. Bloody Mary
contemptuously throws back at Joe the expensive watch
he had given Liat. It breaks at his feet.

Everyone remembers from the musical *South Pacific*
the catchy song "There Is Nothing like a Dame," when
the nurses arrive. The lack of women, the need of fantasy
for young men beleaguered for years in the Pacific, is
one of the principal themes of the novel. Joe Cable's
brief period of passion is preceded and followed by episodes in a lighter key. One concerns another Joe, who
is on a seaplane base in the South Pacific for twenty-
seven months. He and eight hundred other men are
going crazy with stir fever and no action. All are afflicted
with "the itch," a fungus growth in moist areas of the
body, and there is a widespread fear that the Atabrine

tablets they take to counteract malaria will make them impotent. Joe, a simple, well-meaning young man, is still a virgin and has no girl in his life until SeaBee Luther Billis gets a girl to write to him. After a time she announces her marriage, but fortunately Alice Baker of Corvallis, Oregon, takes up the correspondence. Joe is about to send her an unauthorized picture of himself when he receives news of her death in an automobile accident. His response is one of total frustration: "I want to get out of here. I have to get out of here." For Michener, Joe stands for the average guy, with an uncomplicated kind of bravery.

"Passion," which immediately follows "Fo' Dolla'," is an ironic defusing of the passion of Joe Cable's story. Here we are treated to the perplexity of Dr. Paul Benoway, who, after trying to write to his wife about an ordeal he has been through, decides that he has never felt passion. He is convinced of this when he is asked to censor a letter from Tim Hewitt to his wife. The letter is full of explicit prurient detail about their lovemaking, "absolutely clinical," as Dr. Benoway remarks uncomfortably. To his rebuke that letters such as this are not written by ladies and gentlemen, Hewitt's answer is that his letters describe "what we got married for"—something, incidentally, that he had had to teach his wife. Benoway returns to his own letter, gets nowhere, takes time out to read Bill Harbison's apparently passionate letter to his own wife, full of fancy assurances of affection (even though he is currently having an affair). Suddenly Dr. Benoway copies Harbison's rhetoric in place of a prosaic second page of his own letter and sends off an unaccustomed passionate outpouring. It's a form of deception, but it makes him feel good.

"Those Who Fraternize" focuses on the central passional experience of the military in the Pacific: attraction to native or half-caste women, a problem summed up late in the novel by a sailor who wants to know what the other guys "honestly think about chop-suey lovin'? You think it's all right?" "Those who Fraternize" skims over uncomfortable questions of that kind for demonstrations of the allure of four of the De Becque sisters, of the fascination of the half-caste, of the terrible tug-of-war between the familiar and the exotic, and of course of the underlying desperation and pragmatic calculation of the women as they seek security. Bus Adams is the narrator of this episode. He, the favored lover of Latouche Barzan, finds himself superseded by Tony Fry, though Latouche compassionately provides Adams with a substitute. This section is not an idyll, though there is real passion. Rather it is an expression of need on both sides, with an ambiguous qualification when the question arises whether Latouche is also the proprietor of the two brothels on the island, one for enlisted men and one for officers only.

The last four sections of *Tales of the South Pacific* deal with the central military operation up to which it has been leading: the attack on Kuralei. It is a tougher ordeal than has been anticipated. There is an almost minute-by-minute account of the American assault on Green Beach and on dubiously named Sonova Beach. The narrator is there and personally involved, but the narration is matter-of-fact, without rhetoric or emotion. A transport carrying LARU-8 is hit while he is onshore. Many of his friends are killed. There is no time for lament. And after it is over, the soldiers' response is laconic. When asked if the landing was as tough as he had expected, one of them, after long consideration, replies, "No." But then he adds, "But it wasn't no pushover, neither." And with typical defensive deflationary commentary, another soldier says: "You thank your lucky stars you ain't goin' up against the Krauts. That's big league stuff!"

One of the virtues of this book is its unpretentiousness. It does not try to tell what war in the Pacific was like on a grand strategic scale. It does not depict heroic action in the hyperbolic sense. Rather it is a learning experience, both for the reader and for the tens of thousands of military personnel whom the few fictional characters represent. Like Nellie Forbush and Joe Cable they had to plunge into a new world and new circumstances, were forced to question, if not abandon, the old verities by which they had lived and to which they expected to return. Neither totally self-abnegating nor totally self-seeking, not finding life always exciting or always boring, these people and their actions give a satisfying insight into the war in the Pacific, which by reason of its dispersion among many islands remains enveloped in some mystery. As Michener told John P. Hayes, "I knew in my heart, I think, that when the war was over people would want a record of what had happened and how."[2]

Modest as it is, *Tales of the South Pacific* serves that purpose. It was a good beginning for an embryo novelist, but Pulitzer Prize or not, it was only a beginning.

Though Michener had vowed not to write again about foreign lands, he was quickly drawn back to Asia and the South Pacific. In 1951, only four years after his first novel, he published *Return to Paradise*. This is definitely not a novel, but, "a kind of book that—so far as I know—had never been tried before. Such an adventure would make the return to the Pacific intellectually honorable," says Michener in apology. In addition to fear of repeating himself, the author was afraid of disillusionment with the idyllic islands. That did not happen.

The volume is a combination of essays and of stories rather vaguely on the themes of the essays, covering the island areas of the South Pacific and reaching beyond to New Zealand and Australia. Quite properly the first essay is entitled "The Atoll." Like the more famous and more elaborate introduction to *Hawaii*, it tells of the building up of new fragments of earth and celebrates the coral lagoon as "one of the incomparable visual images of the world," ranking with the Pyramids at dawn, the Grand Tetons at dusk, and gleaming arctic wastes. Michener asserts that to say that men have died disillusioned on Pacific islands is "merely to point out that on a lonely atoll, as in most cities, good men find loneliness, weak men find evil." The accompanying story, "Mr. Morgan," illustrates this point, not altogether convincingly. Some men, Michener explains, come to the islands to make a life, but others "come like birds of passage. They think it's part of growing up."

The thirty-page essay "Polynesia" says that "these trivial islands have imposed on history the most lasting vision of the earthly paradise." Tahiti surpasses Bali and Capri as a symbol of hedonistic delight. Yet Polynesia could not escape the ravages of white civilization; it was doomed even before the white men came. While Michener approves of mixed marriages as a way to develop a new and vital Polynesia, the accompanying story, "Povenaaa's Daughter," shows the disillusionment that comes to a native girl as she seeks such a marriage with an American. In the end she wisely accepts marriage with Kim Sing, a Chinese.

Many of the essays and stories touch on how colonial powers govern in these out-of-the-way places. Except for the French, these powers encourage racism. The most vitriolic statement on the subject is in Michener's own person and unexpectedly shows a strong racial antagonism. Writing about Fiji, he calls it a paradise that has been destroyed by the interloping immigrants from India. "They are suspicious, vengeful, whining, unassimilated, provocative aliens in a land where they have lived for more than seventy years. They hate everyone . . ." But he has to admit that Fiji was hell on earth under native and buccaneer rule. He admits too that the Indians have done on Fiji what Americans "have done around the world: they have worked and made things grow."

Two of the islands Michener revisited were scenes of important action in the Pacific war. He describes what Guadalcanal, in the Solomons group, was like for soldiers in battle. Now it is "A quiet, sleeping place of great beauty. It was not always so." On the nearby islet of Mono, Michener describes a settlement called Bali-ha'i, "a filthy, unpleasant village" that he had encountered during the war. He made a note of the name for "its musical quality." (Rodgers and Hammerstein liked it too.) He recalls that during the fighting not one white man was betrayed to the Japanese by the Solomon Islanders. To Michener "The entire island is a monument to the courage of free men who threw back the rampaging enemy." He says he "was moved to deep spiritual excitement" when he saw Guadalcanal again and feels it will always have "a unique place in American history." As for Espiritu Santo there is a good description of what it was like and what war made it become. It was definitely a gainer from the war, since it had been a hellhole before.

Probably the most memorable pairing in the book is the essay on New Zealand and the fifty-four-page story "Until They Sail." "A good deal of hypocrisy obscures realities," Michener asserts, as far as race relations are concerned in this "radical-conservative country." However, the situation is far better than in the United States. The story depicts the tug-of-war between tradition and vital life that comes to the surface under the stress of war. A navy family at Christchurch undergoes dispersion and death. The daughters face the emptiness of life with the men all away. Then the Americans come. One daughter falls in love with an American, but he is killed on Tarawa. In time she is received into his family in the United States, and after her baptism of pain she is ready to emerge into a new life.

Michener's overall assessment is that the South Pacific is not a paradise, but it is a wonderful place in which to live and it is unforgettable to anyone who has absorbed its beauty and its strangeness. He has learned that nature in that region is "so awesome that it compels attention. Other things being roughly equal, that man lives most keenly when he lives in closest harmony with nature."

Rascals in Paradise (1957), written in collaboration with A. Grove Day of the University of Hawaii, is further testimony of Michener's obsession with the Pacific. It is undoubtedly the weakest of his books. The authors' avowed purpose is to examine the lives of "certain strong-natured adventurers" who fled to the Pacific, to see what motivated them, and to find out if the islands of the Pacific are a possible refuge in the atomic age. Accounts are provided of ten such adventurers, of varying motivations, covering a period from 1595 to 1953. These ten exhibits have little in common except that they were all fairly well-known in the Pacific. The individual accounts are badly organized, with much unnecessary material, and are not sufficiently dramatic. The prime effect of this work is less to demonstrate motivation than to prove that the Pacific past is as full of legend as is that of Europe. The book, however, has the curious effect of deflating legend, for in demonstrating bestiality and depravity beyond the reach of legendary European figures it certainly proves that paradise in the Pacific does not exist.

The Floating Island—Japanese Art

When Michener published *Iberia* in 1968 he was careful to note that Spain had not supplanted Japan in his affections. As examples of cultures of dignity and continuity they were, and no doubt are still, equal in his regard. Even Michener, however, has not had the temerity to try to encompass the complexity of Japanese culture in a novel, though *Sayonara* is about Americans in Japan. Wisely he has approached that interest obliquely and tentatively through the study of Japanese art and a valiant effort to make it known to a broad Western public. He published four books in that field from 1955 to 1962.

Michener began in the early 1950s to assemble a collection of Japanese prints, which was speedily enlarged by a bequest and by the opportunity to purchase the Charles H. Chandler Collection. By 1959 Michener had about 5,400 examples of this art form, a superb collection, which he placed in the Honolulu Arts Museum on permanent loan. As the years have gone on he has transferred more than half of the collection to museum ownership, and title to the rest will be transferred in the process of time. Segments of the collection have already been sent on tour to major museums of the world. Michener is certainly correct in his expectation that his efforts in behalf of Japanese art will be long remembered.

It should be pointed out, nevertheless, that for over a century Japanese art in general, and Japanese prints in particular, have been highly regarded by connoisseurs in the West. Painters like Whistler, Manet, and Degas were affected by Japanese artistic manner and even subject; Mary Cassatt, an American Impressionist, early formed a large collection of prints. It seems that the prints of everyday life were so little regarded in Japan that they were used as packing paper for Japanese porcelains. It was in that manner that they came to Western attention and praise in the 1850s and 1860s. Liberty's store in London actively pushed Japanese art after 1862. Edmond de Goncourt, a French novelist and collector, wrote books about Utamaro and Hokusai, two of the leading Japanese printmakers. Moreover, Michener was not alone in his enthusiasm after World War II. Hundreds of thousands of servicemen let loose upon Japan exhausted the supply of objets d'art to bring home souvenirs. Screens and scrolls almost vanished from the country. Prints were fortunately more numerous, though fragile. In any case, interest in them was well established before Michener's first book came out. His works legitimatized that interest and extended it.

What he popularized are known as *ukiyo-e*, or woodblock prints, some of which have a considerable resemblance to genre pictures of Pieter Brueghel. When they were first produced, such prints were in contrast and competition with the conventional illustrations of pietistic cast that had been long in existence. The early woodblock prints were bought for decoration or for use as charms (one of them if hung upside down was guaranteed to keep babies from crying after midnight). After the massacres of Christians in 1638, many Japanese households found it prudent to have a Buddha print on display. Then around 1680 the first of nearly a hundred satirical secular themes were attempted. The scenes to be observed on the Tokkaido road, the imperial roadway between the capitals of Kyoto and Edo (Tokyo), were of paramount importance. These were called *Otsu-e*; that is, pictures made at Otsu on that road. So popular were these scenes that they were commemorated in a street song, "Otsu-e-Bushi."

While *ukiyo-e* designate a "floating world," they were a far cry from "the sad, floating, evanescent, grief-stricken world" of the Buddhist prints. Thus the term soon came to apply to "something like the modern mode, the passing scene, the floating world of pleasure." While the most important artists, such as Hokusai and Hiroshige, did chiefly landscapes, in common usage *ukiyo-e* refers primarily to paintings or woodblock prints that show scenes of everyday life, with a considerable emphasis on beautiful women and actors. As James W. Foster describes it, there were connotations of stylishness and wit, of bawdiness and unconventional patterns of behavior, with a special emphasis on the Kabuki theater.[3]

To Michener's mind this art is distinctive in the same way or to the same degree as that of Siena, which he studied in 1931 and planned to write about, "a confined art" with endlessly repeated iconography. Japanese prints, which he encountered about that same time, he found to be "a more artistic art" and closer to the modern mind because they had

a fuller reference to modern life than that provided by the exquisite gold-leaf work of Siena. For better or worse, the last two hundred years have witnessed the irresistible upthrusting of great masses of people from what used to be the lower social orders.

The *ukiyo-e* reflect this movement more closely than any other art form except the American popular song from Tin Pan Alley. It is Michener's judgment that in two centuries of vigorous life, from 1650 to 1850—which correspond with the life of the Tokunaga shogunate—the Japanese produced "the finest woodblock printing ever achieved." This he demonstrates in his lavishly illustrated volumes presenting the work of the masters of this form. *The Floating World: The Story of Japanese Prints* (1954) has sixty-five illustrations, of which forty are in color. *Japanese Prints: From the Early Masters to the Modern* appeared in 1959. It was supplemented by *The Hokusai Sketchbooks: Selections from the Manga* (1958), selected and edited by Michener.

His fourth volume, *The Modern Japanese Print* (1962), attests to the continued vitality of the print under the influence of Western artists. In a *Horizon* article in May 1960, "An Eastern Art Goes Western" (containing reproductions of outstanding modern prints), Michener points out that there has been a reciprocal influence between East and West. Koshiro Onchi, a modernist in the print form, has said, "My teachers were Wassily Kandinsky, Oskar Kokoschka, and those Van Gogh exhibitions in 1913 and 1914." Edvard Munch, the Norwegian painter, was also influential. Though the Japanese public has taken a conservative stand against innovation, Michener maintains that the fifty or so contemporary artists are successfully maintaining one of Japan's characteristic arts through a fusion of "the best of the international style with the permanent components of a traditional Japanese method."

It is possible to argue a slight connection between Michener's passion for Japanese art and his 1954 novel, *Sayonara*, for the latter does depict the world of the theater as the Japanese half of an intercultural love affair. This was a major and valid subject for fiction in the years during and after World War II, especially during the occupation of Japan. An interesting variation of it appears in the much later *Hawaii*, where the problem is the marriage of a sophisticated girl from metropolitan Japan to an uncultivated though worthy Nisei of working-class origins in Hawaii. The Hawaiian marriage does not work; the girl goes back to her own civilization with regret but relief. In *Sayonara* the conflict is external but no less immediate. There are too many barriers, and on the whole the feeling is that such marriages should be discouraged, though at the same time the reader feels deep sympathy for the two couples whose problems are central to the novel. The minor case is that of an enlisted man, Joe Kelly, who in spite of tremendous obstacles placed in his way by the military does marry Katsumi, a plain but very loving peasant. Finally, when he is ordered home and forced to leave his pregnant wife behind, the couple commit suicide, ironically only weeks before the American regulations will be relaxed.

The central characters are a famous Air Force ace, Major Lloyd Gruver, son of a general and himself a West Point graduate, and Hana-ogi, an equally famous member of the Takarazuka Theater. As an actress she is under a discipline at least equal to that which Gruver must accept. Love, of course, finds a way. They live together, thereby inviting further harassment by the military and cautionary restraint by the head of the theater. Ultimately both of them succumb to the demands of their disciplines, and though love has not cooled, they go their separate professional ways. (In the movie drawn from the novel Marlon Brando comes back to an impossible "lived happily ever after" conclusion.)

One of the focuses of the novel is the stupidity of the American reaction to mixed marriages, equating it with a general racism reinforced by hatred toward a recent enemy. There is also evident a jealousy on the part of American women, notably a brigadier general's wife and the mother of the girl to whom Gruver is engaged. All of these characters are wooden and unconvincing, part of the furniture of an uncivil obstacle course.

Although *Sayonara* makes no attempt to grapple with the complexities of Japanese culture, it almost inevitably gives some praise for and insight into that life. (The novel was published some months before Michener met Mari Yoriko Sabusawa.) Major Gruver says:

I concluded that no man could comprehend women until he had known the women of Japan with their unbelievable combination of unremitting work, endless suffering and boundless warmth.

The contrast of the Japanese women with army wives is devastating, though on reflection the reader is likely to feel the exhibits on either side are too stereotyped.

Japanese art as a key to Japanese feeling has an important part in this novel. There is a chapter in which Gruver and Hana-ogi go to a museum in Kyoto to look at prints, forty-one of them, of the original actress called Hana-ogi. He is disappointed and thinks them ugly, even one by Utamaro. The museum official takes him to task for his incomprehension of Japanese artistic conventions, their sense of form and color. In a corner of the Utamaro print are a few characters constituting a poem that can be read in many ways. This is the essence of Japanese art: "Our life in Japan is one of implied meanings, hidden significances." The novel itself conveys something of that elusive quality. Gruver is almost mesmerized by the sight of the Takarazuka girls passing along a flower walk and over a bridge, "by the poetic swaying of their long green skirts and the lithe, hidden movements of their beautiful bodies as they passed into darkness." On another occasion, he suddenly feels as if he were "in a world of swirling darkness where the only reality was this earth—this earth of Japan."

Clearly one of the goals Michener set for himself in his writing about the Orient was to bring Americans to a better understanding and appreciation of Japanese life. This was a task of importance, for feeling against the Japanese, in the Pacific Coast states as well as among the men fighting in the Pacific, understandably ran very high. (Those who, in the background, read Japanese mail, so to speak, often found themselves sympathetic toward the trials and uncertainties of the Japanese with whom they became acquainted in this way—to the disgust if not the active aggression of servicemen to whom they expressed such sympathy.) A compensating weight of feeling came, however, from those who, later, served in the occupying forces and became enamored not of the *dolce far niente* of the South Seas but of the remarkably disciplined, uncomplaining behavior of a defeated people who in their travail still had time to respond to the beauty of nature and artistic objects.

During the early 1950s Michener published a half-dozen articles about Japan in such popular magazines as *Reader's Digest*, *Holiday*, *The Ladies' Home Journal*, and *Life*. It is likely that for tens of thousands of American readers these articles were the first intimation that there was something to be admired about Japan. Some of the articles were simple human-interest stories. In *Life* for February 21, 1955, Michener gives a detailed account of a mixed marriage with many photographs. A young soldier, who had been a slaughterhouse worker in Chicago before the war, had gone to Japan in September 1945 and shortly had fallen in love with a girl whom he observed on the street. They married Japanese-style and lived with her family, though they could communicate only by gestures. Eighteen months later the U.S. authorities temporarily permitted mixed marriages and the couple were wed at the American consulate in Yokohama. They arrived in Chicago on Christmas Day 1947. The man's family were hospitable and friendly but the mother finally became fed up with noncommunication, with "Jap talk," as she called it. The couple moved out, encountered hostility from neighbors. They moved again to a more friendly neighborhood. The wife went to work in a sweatshop so that her husband could get training as a movie photographer. The wife was admirable for good works and for financial sobriety. No doubt this was too much of a sentimental success story, but it did offer a picture that enlisted sympathy and encouraged understanding. Some months later *Life* (November 7, 1955) had another story with pictures about a mixed marriage, the wedding of James A. Michener and Mari

Yoriko Sabusawa in the Memorial Chapel on the University of Chicago campus.

In August 1956 a Michener article, "Why I Like Japan," appeared in *Reader's Digest*. He cited the reasons why servicemen fall in love with Japan. First was their attraction to the "utterly delectable" Japanese girls. Nonetheless, Michener said that his advice had generally been not to marry, because of the great culture gap to be bridged when the girls reached the United States. A second reason for admiring Japan was the simple, peaceful way of life, "the rare wine of Japanese living." The frigid and formal exterior of the Japanese masked "a warm and even hilarious" inner being, which several million American servicemen had had the good fortune to discover. A third characteristic was a discipline, both personal and social, equaled in no other modern society. The Japanese were stoical, he explained, in suffering, did their duty with no display of emotion, were loyal to Japan, to the Emperor, and to their immediate superiors, and conducted themselves with exquisite politeness. Theirs was an "extraordinary love of beauty"; Japan was "a place where art lives in the streets"; the most simple and functional object was a thing of beauty. Though the public face of towns and streets was generally ugly and dilapidated, to their inhabitants this was a matter of minor importance. "In the home is where true beauty lives," they would say.

There were certainly strains and stresses in postwar Japan. "Madam Butterfly in Bobby Sox" (*Reader's Digest*, October 1956) discussed this in terms of the emancipation of women, which was perhaps the most important legacy of the MacArthur proconsulship. The liberation of women "shook Japan worse than the 1923 earthquake." Michener told that during his first seven trips to Japan he met only one Japanese wife socially. Now the situation was changing and he ventured to predict that the freedom of women and their involvement in public affairs would probably save Japan from the blandishments of communism.

None of Michener's magazine commentaries were profound. Neither the articles nor *Sayonara* had more than a temporary communicative value. But they made it possible for millions of readers to reconsider their stereotypes about Japan—if they wished. And the books on Japanese art are permanent testimony about enduring Japanese greatness.

Hawaii

"From the Boundless Deep," the opening section of *Hawaii* (1959), the first of Michener's big novels, is a paean to the forces of nature, which are grand but not necessarily beneficent. It is a brilliant description of the process by which islands in the Pacific are created: emergence by volcanic action, build-up of coral reefs, subsidence, reemergence, more tireless building of coral, in a cycle repeated for millions and millions of years. "In violence the island lived, and in violence a great beauty was born." There is "Ceaseless life and death, endless expenditure of beauty and capacity, tireless ebb and flow and rising and subsidence of the ocean." In the two-thousand-mile chain from which the Hawaiian Islands grew "every sequential step in the process of life and death" could have been witnessed.

Before these islands had finished growing, civilizations had developed in distant lands. By contrast these islands were truly new: "They were raw. They were empty. They were waiting." But they were barren of amenity. They lacked even the coconut, though they did have the sandalwood, the tree of death. These beautiful, inhospitable islands were waiting for "a new breed of men to invade them with food and courage and determination." There had never been on earth a place that "even began to compete with these islands in their capacity to encourage natural life to develop freely and radically up to its own potential."

At the end of this proem we realize that it has been related by a first-person narrator, whose "I" will pop up at intervals throughout the novel, but who will remain unidentified until the last page. He is Hoxworth Hale, born in 1898, and therefore getting on toward sixty as the novel ends at the beginning of 1955. To a degree he must be considered a reluctant witness to the process of development of which he speaks, though since we know nothing about him, his bias as observer cannot be known until the end, when we see the new breed of men for whom the islands have been waiting—"the Golden Men," as he calls them. By that time we realize that the new breed is an amalgamation of various strains in a process that is promising but by no means complete. It is even possible that the four men whom Hale denominates as "Golden Men" are not worthy of that description, especially as he egoistically places himself in that category.

What is important in the novel is the epic quality of the coming to Hawaii of four major successive human strains: the first Polynesian settlers from the region of Bora Bora and Tahiti; the American missionaries from New England and their godless sailor counterparts; Chinese peasants from two neighboring but antagonistic villages in South China; and Japanese peasants from Hiroshima prefecture. While the Polynesians arrived at some time in the ninth century—around the time the sons of Charlemagne were dividing up his kingdom—the main action of the story, beginning a thousand years later with the arrival of the missionaries in successive waves, demonstrates the gradual transformation of the Hawaiian body and mind.

Though this is the first of Michener's panchronic novels, on the whole he surmounts his structural prob-

lems well. The basic strategy is to create characters who
will embody recognizable characteristics of people of a
particular region living at a given time, and who by
their interaction will carry the developmental theme
along. The great problem is how to keep the vast number of characters who are spread over many generations
in some kind of intelligible order. Michener meets the
problem by the artifice of repetition of family names,
even in mixed marriages, and by the placing of elaborate
genealogical charts at the end of the book. (The reader
has to consult them frequently.)

Michener's first penetration of the past—the Polynesian past—is the most unified and the most dramatic, because it is controlled only by legend and
probability. On Bora Bora, loveliest of islands, there
occurs a power struggle in which the high priest of Oro,
a new and fierce god, intimidates King Tamatoa and
finally forces him and his brother Teroro to flee. A new
temple to Oro is being consecrated on neighboring Havaiki. The king and his leaders must attend, and sacrifice
eight men. Naturally those chosen are the ones who
have offended the high priest or whose death will be an
affront to the king.

After the ceremony the Bora Bora leaders realize
that they must seek a new home. They and their ad-
herents select roots and saplings for the new land, carry
brood sows with them, and allow only women capable
of bearing children to accompany them. Teroro is thus
forced to leave his wife Marama behind. "They fled at
night with no drums beating," an unheroic exit, a
confession of failure; but before such a departure they
had made a raid on Havaiki and killed the king who
wished to rule over them. Then, with only traditions
of voyaging for guidance, they set forth on what turns
out to be a month-long voyage. A great storm carries
them far off their planned course; they are unable to put
in anywhere for water and supplies. The first death oc-

curs on the seventeenth day. On the twenty-seventh day, after a long leg to the northwest, they see evidence of land and soon reach a mountainous island that reaches to heaven itself. There the goddess of volcanoes, Tere, manifests her displeasure at having been left behind (they have at any rate dumped Oro overboard), and they are forced to move from their first landing to an area on the western part of the island where Kona is now located. They call this new land Havaiki, a name often invoked by the ancient Polynesians as they sought utopia.

Although Teroro urges that a new start be made in their society now that they have rid themselves of Oro, they set up a temple where the rainbow ends and think it expedient to sacrifice one slave in an ancient rite. Also by ancient custom King Tamatoa lies with his sister. A strictly hierarchical society is established, protected by rigid tabus, a structure that will last basically unchanged for a thousand years, since no white men will impinge upon it until the arrival of Captain Cook in 1778 and the event of the unification of all the islands under King Kamehameha shortly thereafter.

This sketchy account of its Polynesian origins is a given, imbued with the poetry of myth, against which the later recorded events of Hawaiian history will be played out. Implicit in the description is the immobility of culture patterns, a complete lack of economic drive, an essential hedonism, and, shocking to the Western World, a happy sexual promiscuity. The Hawaiians have warm, loving natures, an embrace as wide as they can reach in spirit, a love based on simple animistic religious belief. They think of children, whom they value highly, as belonging to them all. The one-time drive and capacity for adaptation that brought them to the islands are not sustained. They settle back into simple, unambitious enjoyment, the mass of the people supporting and controlled by the *alii*—that is, the aristocrats—who are people of tremendous height and girth and who are themselves content with the old ways. It is not difficult to infer, even in advance of the evidence, that these people will be incapable of survival in a world dominated by new ways and new ideas, just as they will be incapable of surviving the measles virus.

The title of the next section, "From the Farm of Bitterness," gives advance warning about one quality of missionaries. It is basically a starved and sterile belief that they bring, though fortunately it is capable of softening by cross-culturation, if the process be allowed to exist. We encounter Abner Hale and John Whipple as divinity students at Yale, a haven of Calvinistic Congregationalism. They receive spiritual illumination when Keoki Kanaloa, a six-foot-five Hawaiian, tells of pagan practices and the sacrifices of human victims on the island of Maui. The two young men promptly apply to the Commission for Foreign Missions to be sent to Hawaii. Whipple, who is training also in medicine, is just what they want; Hale is characterized by one of the commission's ministers as "an offensive, undernourished, sallow-faced little prig, the kind that wrecks any mission to which he is attached." Nonetheless the head of the board accepts Hale and arranges a marriage with his niece Jerusha Bromley, from a cultivated and gentle background, because he wants to make sure that she will have a godly mate. The uncle is guilty also on the wedding day of concealing the arrival of a letter to Jerusha from Rafer Hoxworth, a sea captain, who has intended to marry her. All this intrigue about Jerusha is somewhat contrived, but with the suitable purpose of introducing into *Hawaii* the affectional antithesis of Abner Hale.

On September 1, 1821, eleven couples, nine of them just married, set forth from Boston for Hawaii on the tiny brig *Thetis*, under the command of Captain Retire Janders. The regulations governing their mission are precise. Property is to be held in common. There is to be no interference in the government of the islands. Their charge is to bring the heathen to Christ: "You are to aim at nothing less than the complete regeneration and salvation of a society." Needless to say, it is Reverend Abner Hale who will interpret these admonitions to mean that there shall be no trafficking with the enemy, no accommodation of heathen practice and belief.

The sixty-page account of the voyage down to and around the tip of South America is remarkably vivid. They encounter a Brazilian slave ship off Cape Verde, and when Hale learns of the existence of slavery in Hawaii, he vows that he will eradicate that practice. Rounding Cape Horn is an agonizing effort. Failing to make that passage, they fall back upon the Strait of Magellan, which is even more agonizing, for they are forty-two days in the strait before emerging into the Pacific. Just one evidence of the ambiguity of the forces that govern the universe is the fact that the ship cannot make it through the strait with a gale behind it; it can only complete the passage by tacking into a wind from the west. Another ambiguity, of which Hale learns later, is that the sinful Captain Hoxworth makes it around Cape Horn in three days.

Abner begins his missionary activities on board ship. He starts to learn Hawaiian almost at the beginning of the voyage. He attempts to convert the seamen on board, to Captain Janders' extreme annoyance. He forces the captain to throw sinful novels—all novels are sinful—overboard in fulfillment of a vow, when they finally do emerge into the Pacific. He is eager to go on board other ships to conduct services for their sailors. On the last of these occasions the ship turns out to be the *Carthaginian*, captained by Hoxworth. When he discovers that Abner is the man who took Jerusha away from him, there is a fighting confrontation in which Hale goes overboard as Hoxworth curses him and hopes that he will be eaten by sharks. Before Hale is rescued, a shark does graze

him in an Achilles tendon. He limps ashore at Lahaina
on Maui, where naked native women have swum joyously out to the ship, his introduction to a new and
sinful world.

While of necessity the other islands figure later in
the novel, for the time being it is Maui that is the center
of action. Keoki's mother, Malama, is the *Alii Nui*, a
kind of princess-priestess, the person from whom mana
flows. The nineteenth wife of King Kamehameha, she
is also married to Kelolo, her younger brother. She is
six feet four; he is six feet seven. They are descended
from Marama and Teroro of the first two migrations
(Teroro went back for Marama) and bear their names,
which have been subjected to phonetic change.

Malama is massively swung aboard the ship when
it arrives in harbor. Overflowing with love for the mission women, she immediately decides to dress in Western style and orders them to make her a dress, or rather
a tent, as it turns out. She is not entirely receptive to
the religious teaching of the missionaries: "We have our
own gods. It is the words, the writing that we need."
She compromises and gives only half her time to in-
struction in reading and writing. She respects Hale, for
of all who have so far come to Lahaina only he has
brought more than he has taken away. But she finds his
notion of Christian humility hard to understand, since
he is guilty of pride and is convinced that what he orders
is necessarily what the Lord has commanded. Malama
is received as a Christian only when she dies. She is
given Christian burial; however, her brother-husband
and her son surreptitiously give her true burial with all
the pagan rites, including Kelolo's mutilation of one of
his eyes.

In spite of their generous welcome, the missionaries
have a hard time. As the narrative voice points out:

Actually no missionaries in history had so far visited a gentler
or finer group of people than these Hawaiians. They were

clean, free from repulsive tropical diseases, had fine teeth, good manners, a wild joy in living, and they had devised a well-organized society; but to Abner they were vile.

Perhaps for him the image of their vileness was the daughter of Malama, naked Noelani, surfing joyously out to the ships. She was "a terrifying vision, the personification of all they had come to conquer. Her nakedness was a challenge, her beauty a danger, her way of life an abomination and her existence an evil." In spite of stern warning she marries her brother Keoki and has a child by him. Though Jerusha saves Noelani's child from death during the measles epidemic, the island woman refuses ever to become a Christian, at least not under Abner's auspices. In due time she gladly marries Rafer Hoxworth—a further abomination in the eyes of the Lord—and becomes one of the major progenitors of the new Hawaiians.

Only three of the missionaries have an active part in the story, three quite different personalities representing various aspects of the life of the newcomers. The wife of Abraham Hewlett dies in childbirth. After some years the missionaries are summoned to a meeting in Honolulu to expel him from their ranks because he has married a native woman. It was, in fact, John Whipple who married the couple, for which he is reprimanded by the meeting. He resigns in disgust and comes to Lahaina to join Captain Janders in a business venture. Hewlett later joins Hoxworth in a similar activity. As has often been said in derision, the missionaries came to do good and did well. The novel observes, further, that the missionaries love the Hawaiians as "potential Christians" but "despise them as people." Whipple takes the opposite position on principle as well as on pragmatic grounds. Hewlett merely accedes to inner necessity. Indeed, the major charge of this section of the novel is the lack of love on the part of the missionaries as represented

by Abner Hale. Even Dr. Thorne, Jerusha's uncle, is
displeased by Hale's attitudes when he comes on a visit
of inspection, for Hale's position is not in harmony with
the diminished Calvinism of the Congregational Church.
Hale has prepared no one for ordination, and it is Thorne
who ordains two Hawaiians brought from Honolulu.
Thorne, in fact, fears that Hale has done more harm
than good, as he takes Micah and the other Hale children
off to Boston to complete their secondary education in
preparation for Yale.

It is John Whipple who emerges as the right kind
of emissary of an alien culture because of his tolerant
understanding of the Hawaiians, because of his basically
scientific attitude and method, and because of his acute
business sense. It is nowhere suggested that *all* that was
needed was to improve the physical and economic environment, but certainly the physical basis of Hawaiian
life needed improvement, as a result of which they could
achieve a better spiritual condition.

Rafer Hoxworth starts out as the villainous wild
man of the Pacific. He is guilty of unrestrained physical
action when aroused sexually or egoistically. He appears
to consider all non-Americans a lesser breed, whatever
his incidental pleasure in their women. But he is capable
of goodwill. It is he who brings and sets up the New
England farmhouse for Jerusha. He is tempered by the
influence of Noelani. He meets a kind of comeuppance
when in 1849–50 young Micah Hale, fresh from divinity
school at Yale, is prevailed upon to sail from San Francisco on Hoxworth's ship. Micah and Hoxworth's
daughter Malama fall in love and are married by the
captain after Micah has stood up to him. It is Hoxworth's judgment that the young man has too much
get-up-and-go long to remain a minister. He is right,
for predictably Abner Hale considers his son's marriage
an abomination. Micah resigns from the ministry and

becomes Hoxworth's partner. Thereafter the H & H flag is known around the world.

The narrative dealing with Chinese immigrants to Hawaii goes back as far as the one dealing with its Polynesian origins. This is in many ways a sharp contrast, a contrast between indefatigable ambition bred in a poverty-stricken environment and the lotus-land indolence of the South Seas. There is, furthermore, uncomfortable artifice in having the saga of the Chinese in Hawaii dominated by the personality of Nyuk Tsin, who lives for 106 years.

The ancient history of the Chinese immigrants is epic in tone and is contemporary with the flight from Bora Bora. By reason of drought and famine as well as because of the incursions of Tartars, peasants in the rich farmland of Honan province are forced to abandon their village and migrate south under the leadership of a fellow townsman, who is a general. The great march of 857–74 is made by starving men and women from the village and those who join them along the way, as well as by the thousand children born on the march. These people are highly disciplined and are able to hold to old customs when they arrive at their new home, where they are obliged to occupy the less fertile highlands, leaving the lowlands to alien types from the South. The highlanders are called Hakku, the lowlanders Punti. For a thousand years they live side by side with practically no friendly contact. The Hakku do not bind their women's feet, a cause of disdain on the part of the Punti. There is no mixed marriage between the two communities, especially after a Punti ran away with a Hakku woman in 1693, causing a feud to develop.

With this background we leap to the middle of the nineteenth century. Nyuk Tsin—Perfect Jade—is born in 1847, when Hakku fortunes are degenerating. Her father becomes a warrior and dies; her mother is shot.

She is captured by four men and inducted into prostitution. Down in the Punti village in 1865 there is great excitement when Kee Chun Fat, a member of the Kee family, arrives home after a sojourn in California. He summons a relative, Kee Mun Ki, who is cook in a brothel in Macao, and urges him to better himself by going to America. In April 1865 Dr. John Whipple comes to the area in search of workers for the Hawaiian fields. He visits both villages and, to the annoyance of Chun Fat, insists that half of the imported workers be Hakku, whom he finds to resemble his conservative New England forebears. Hakku women will be permitted by their people to go to Hawaii, but not Punti women. All the Punti men must marry before they set out, Kee Mun Ki among them. (It will be allowable for them to marry in Hawaii too, for in this way they will work harder; but they must never fail to send money home to their village.) Sexually exhausted, an immigrant band of three hundred set out from Hong Kong, among them Nyuk Tsin, who is being sent from a Macao brothel to a similar establishment in Honolulu in Kee Mun Ki's charge.

This voyage too is memorable, because of the inhumanity of Captain Hoxworth, who makes all three hundred and one of the Chinese sleep in the hold with no fresh air, little food, and no sanitary facilities. Whipple comes to their defense and wins some concessions from the intractable Hoxworth by threatening to write about him all over the world.

Hawaii is jubilant when the Chinese arrive, for it is understood that they will go home when their contracts expire, since there are no women available. *The Hawaiian Mail* remarks that they are "infinitely superior to the shiftless Hawaiians," news that is not calculated to endear the newcomers to the natives. The Punti do think in terms of a temporary stay, but the Hakku think: "This is a good land to make a home in, and we shall never leave." Kee Mun Ki, enamored of Nyuk Tsin, refuses to hand her over to the brothelkeeper, going so far as to refund the purchase price to him. Whipple is brought into the altercation that takes place and is so impressed by Kee and his supposed wife that he employes them in his own home. Kee is stubborn and bright. He gets $2.50 a week, and Mrs. Whipple voluntarily raises Nyuk Tsin's pay to $1.00 a week. The Chinese woman is also allowed an acre of land on which to farm for her own benefit in her off hours at night.

The land on which these imported laborers are to work is "more bleak and barren than that which they had fled in China." Ninety percent of the fields around Honolulu are desert because of the lack of rainfall. Even the Hoxworth acreage from the last *Alii Nui* is "practically worthless, thirsting for water." In a response that is to become characteristic of Chinese settlers, they are all eager to get back to Honolulu: they are city folk, destined to make their way in the city, in time to a great extent to *be* the city. Whipple, always compassionate and eager to enrich the Hawaiian race, concludes that they have become part of Hawaii and should be educated, should initiate new industries, should become fellow citizens. Through them the dying Hawaiian race will be regenerated. The reaction of right-thinking people, however, is simple and dramatic: "The Sonofabitch ought to be horse-whipped."

Because Kee has an official wife in China, Nyuk Tsin recedes modestly into the background as the designated aunt of her own children, and up to the time of her death, long after the presumed death of wife number one, she insists that remittances be sent regularly to the Punti village. Her husband is obdurate about refusing to let her buy land that Whipple is willing to let her have, because they are going back to China, but she knows that she will not go back and, later, devotes all her energies to seeing to it that her children get a superior education, not, of course, at elite Punahou School but at a lesser institution where individualistic Uliassutai Karakoram Blake (a historical figure) grooms them for a constructive life. The great question is, finally, which son will receive the bulk of family support so that he can go on to Harvard. The one chosen is Africa Kee, who in time becomes the mainstay of the whole family.

In 1870, however, it is no longer possible to conceal from Dr. Whipple that Kee has leprosy. Nyuk Tsin and her husband hide out for a while with the connivance of sympathetic Hawaiians, but eventually Kee is caught and forced to go to the leper colony on the island of Molokai. His wife surrenders her children to other families and plans to see to it that the fifth child, with whom she is pregnant, be brought back to Honolulu and given away. The inhumane conditions the couple find in the leper colony are beyond belief. The lepers are "thrown ashore with no stores of clothing, no money, no food and no medicine." Nyuk Tsin discovers that

there was no voice of government, no voice of God, no healing medicine. In the houseless peninsula there was not even a secure supply of water, and food was available only when the *Kilauea* [the supply ship] remembered to kick into the sea enough casks and cattle. In truth, the lepers had been thrown ashore with nothing except the sentence of certain death, and what they did until they died no one cared.

As the narrator comments, "For six indifferent years no official in Honolulu found time to concern himself with such problems or allocate even miserly sums for their solution."

The two Chinese newcomers are excluded even from the leper community, such as it is, until the couple succeed in killing Big Saul, a terrorist, when he attempts to rape Nyuk Tsin. After this the Kees receive notice and respect; they have a house of sorts and spiritual peace. After her husband's death Nyuk Tsin runs a sort of hospital.

In 1873, at the age of twenty-six, Nyuk Tsin is allowed to return to Honolulu if doctors there certify that she is free of leprosy. As she leaves Molokai, Father Damien arrives. She gives him her house. In Honolulu she in time finds her fifth son, who has been adopted. To whom does he belong? The two mothers argue and Nyuk Tsin is defeated by love. The child is both Keoki Kanakoa, adopted son of the last governor of Honolulu, and Australia Kee, biological offspring of Chinese parents in Hawaii. It should be added that relinquishing the child is made easier for Nyuk Tsin by his receiving four acres of choice land from the governor.

An historical event of major importance to the Chinese community occurs at the turn of the century, when bubonic plague is brought in on a ship from the Orient. The health authorities have three days of debate before they decide to burn houses in Chinatown. The Hales and the Hewletts and the Whipples volunteer for the dangerous work of checking the area to make sure everyone is out—it is a horrible slum owned by those very families. On January 20, 1900, a large-scale burning accidentally engulfs all of Chinatown. The Chinese think it is an act of discrimination. Why only their part of the city? Nyuk Tsin regenerates courage as she counsels them to buy land: "A city belongs to those who are willing to fight for it." A comment by the narrator tells that the white people—the haoles—never sold land. Therefore Nyuk Tsin's determination to get land at any cost throws her "directly athwart the established wealth of the island."

While the Kees are the center of interest in this long section, the narrative must deal also with the contemporary Hawaiians and haoles. Haole Whipple Hoxworth—"Wild Whip," as he is known—is a throwback to his grandfather Rafer Hoxworth, who had early inducted him into the joys of the brothel. Whip refuses to complete his education and ships out on a Hoxworth vessel at the age of fourteen. After knocking about the world he surreptitiously brings in pineapple plants from Formosa (today Taiwan). He wants to try these plants out on land belonging to Nyuk Tsin. Whip is in continual collision with Micah Hale, "a symbol of rectitude and a man determined not to have the H & H empire sullied by the escapades of his wild young nephew." Whip in return for severing ties with the firm receives 4,000 acres of land, commenting: "Jesus, are you goddamned missionaries going to regret this day!"

Dissidence of a more immediately constructive cast is that of Janders Whipple, who is obsessed with the possibility of irrigating the unproductive land in the islands, especially on Oahu. In the United States he encounters a water engineer named Milton Overpeck, who knows about aquifers. On September 14, 1881, after prolonged drilling they break through rock to gushing water, and a new era of productivity begins. A Janders girl marries the elderly engineer, and the land he has been given in exchange for his expertise returns to "the grand alliance of Hoxworth-Whipple-Hale-Janders-Hewlett."

In 1892, when passage of the McKinley tariff is an overt act of discrimination against Hawaiian sugar, Whip undertakes to foment "the most respectable revolution in history" in order to bring the Kingdom of Hawaii into the United States. As the narrator sums up the monarchy, the Kamehameha line ended in 1872, followed by "amiable but incompetent *alii*." On January 29, 1891, Queen Liliuokalani succeeds her brother and resolutely determines to end the domination of haoles like Micah Hale and his cohorts. She is eager to combat republicanism, Congregationalism, and sugar; to those ends she announces her intention of abrogating the constitution and restoring absolute monarchy. Whip finally manages to enlist Micah's help to combat this, but annexation is frustrated when U.S. sugar interests prevent the treaty from being jammed through a lame duck session of the Senate in 1893. The Queen is deposed. Micah sets up an illiberal territorial government with property qualifications for voting and the exclusion of Orientals from the franchise or elective office. He also excludes Wild Whip from any participation in the new regime. On August 12, 1898, by proclamation of the President (the same McKinley of the tariff act) Hawaii is admitted as a territory—but we are told that "in the islands this happy event seemed more like a funeral than a birth." Malama, Micah's wife, accepts the revolution and annexation on the ground that it is better for "the world to see us dying as we actually were." She asserts, however:

In the end we were pitifully used by a gang of robbers. . . . We poor, generous Hawaiians were abused, lied about, debased in public and defrauded of our nation.

For the Japanese component of future Hawaii, the novel does not go back in time. Rather we observe a small community in Hiroshima prefecture in 1902. The young engage in mating patterns as formal as those of birds. In the case of Kamejiro Sakagawa, aged twenty-two, his approach to Yoko, with whom he sleeps clandestinely and perilously, is broken by the decision to go to Hawaii among a group of 1,850 workmen being imported by Janders & Whipple. A lyrical account of the beauties of the Inland Sea as they depart is balanced by a lyrical description of the island of Kauai, to which many of them go. *The Honolulu Mail* is also lyrical in its assertion that the Japanese are "obedient, extraordinarily clean, law-abiding, not given to gambling and eager to accomplish at least eighty percent more labor than the lazy Chinese ever did."

These workers do in fact toil twelve hours a day for a pay of sixty-seven cents plus board and room. Kamejiro makes additional money by constructing a bathhouse for his fellow workers. His desire to make enough money to return home to marry is continually frustrated by demands made by Japanese agencies. After the Russo-Japanese War comes to a successful conclusion, the loyal emigrants are taken to Honolulu for a celebration and wear Japanese uniforms in a parade. Kamejiro maintains his loyalty to Japanese ways: "Spiritually he was part of Japan, a warrior who had never yet borne arms, but who stood ready to die for his emperor." Finally, in 1915, when he is thirty-three, he decides to send for Yoko, only to find that she has long since married. His mother chooses a wife for him, but the girl refuses to have anything to do with him when he meets her at the boat in workman's clothing. He disconsolately trades wives with his friend Ishii. It turns out that he gets the better wife; like her Chinese counterpart, Yoriko supplements their income by cooking for bachelors. Because he is skilled in the use of dynamite Kamejiro is taken by Whip to Oahu to work on a big reclamation project. He turns down an offer of land, preferring to receive $200 so that he can soon go home. But he gives to others and his repatriation is delayed. Meanwhile four sons, Goro, Tadao, Minoru, and Shigeo, are born, as well as a daughter, Reiko.

Though the parents continue to think of themselves as Japanese who will return home, the children are assimilated, in part at least, to the new culture and develop new allegiances, or at least conflicting ones. In the American school the Sakagawas learn that all men are created equal, but their father teaches them that the Etas (Japanese untouchables) are beyond the pale. In the Shinto school they learn formal Japanese, but at night they drill each other in correct English, and with other children they speak pidgin. The boys are denied entrance to the elite Punahou School on one ground or another until the need for athletes outweighs racism and Tadao is recruited on a full scholarship and will best his brothers and others on the McKinley High School team. There is great rivalry among youthful factions. Tadao is beaten up, but he and his brothers in turn beat up the offending gang. The boys take it as more or less natural that they are "clawing their way up the ladder of island life." Their sister fares less well. Contributions to help Japan in its China war of the 1930s make it impossible for Reiko to go to college. Instead her father sets up a barber shop where she and other Japanese girls are a great attraction, especially to the fleet.

What happens to members of the Sakagawa family after Pearl Harbor is the most illuminating part of this section of the novel. The Japanese in Hawaii were, in fact, treated much better than in California, "where the imaginary danger of trouble from potential fifth columnists was not a fraction of the real danger that could have existed in Hawaii."[4] There is, however, a painful scene in which Yoriko, in strange costume and without the ability to speak English, is rescued from a mob by her sons. (It finally comes out that Kamejiro has refused all overtures to become a citizen because in Japan he is officially married to the girl who turned him down. He cannot endure the loss of face that would occur if he had the record changed in Hiroshima-ken.)

Because of their ambiguous situation and fundamental patriotism Japanese youth in Hawaii flock to the 222nd Combat Team under Colonel Mark Whipple. (This unit, of course, is the fictional equivalent of the famous 442nd that won fame in Italy and elsewhere.) They suffer discrimination at a military camp in Mississippi but are able to bear it in their determination to prove their loyalty. As Goro says: "We fight double. Against the Germans and for every Japanese in America." In the battle for Monte Cassino in January 1944 Goro is commissioned on the field. Later in the war a Texas battalion is trapped in the Vosges and the Japanese go to its rescue. Minoru Sakagawa is killed, as is Colonel

Whipple. Shigeo is made a lieutenant. It costs the lives of 800 Japanese to rescue 341 Texans. The Japanese more than earn their rightful place place in America and in Hawaii.

"The Golden Men" of the last section of the novel are both a recapitulation of the development of the population of Hawaii and a guide and promise to the future. The Hoxworth Hale narrator asserts that he had come to realize that

this bright, hopeful man of the future, this unique contribution of Hawaii to the rest of the world, did not depend for his genius upon racial marriage at all. He was a product of the mind. His was a way of thought, not of birth.

Hoxworth is still conservative, still antilabor. Racially he is mostly haole. Behind him he has the wealth of Hale & Hoxworth to the amount of $200,000,000, and of Janders and Whipple to the extent of $185,000,000. He is a conservative figure with some sense of the opening of new vistas that cannot be avoided. Hong Kong Kee has five children in mainland colleges and two in the Punahou School. He thinks of himself as pure Chinese, "whatever that means." Shigeo Sakagawa, now a captain in the occupation force in Japan, is "the forward cutting edge of a revolution . . . about to break out over Hawaii"; he is a man "stern, incorruptible, physically hard and fearless." Hale has missed the opportunity to co-opt him and others like him into the power structure. Hong Kong is more far-seeing and offers Shigeo a job after he has completed law school.

The last of the Golden Men, Kelly Kanakoa, over six feet, weighing 180 pounds, can trace his ancestors back to King Tamatoa, one hundred and thirty-four generations in the past. He teaches surfing to divorcees who come to Waikiki and is in great demand for more intimate servicing. He lives for the day, a sybarite of sybarites. He becomes acquainted with Elinor Henderson, of mission extraction, who has come to study the past. Her grandfather thought the missionaries were wrong: right god, wrong values. She wants to write an article about Kelly, to be called "The Dispossessed." Kelly takes Elinor home to meet his mother, Malama Kanakoa, who had gone to Vassar. Four gigantic women, a frieze of giants, of mixed extraction but Hawaiian in outlook, are there and readily accept Elinor. Kelly believes it is the missionary progeny who are dispossessed, for Congregationalism has lost out, giving way to Catholicism and Mormonism. A genuine love affair seems to be developing when, picnicking on a beach, Kelly and Elinor are caught by the great tsunami, or earthquake-induced tidal wave, of 1948 and Elinor is killed.

Though *Hawaii* was published more or less simultaneously with the Island's achievement of statehood, and was a festive celebration of that long-desired achievement, the narrative of its last section deals only with the first steps in the process.[5] Opposition comes from various quarters. Native Hawaiians fear that they will lose what is left of their identity. The haole old guard wants no change, especially as it becomes evident that the ruling force will be the Democratic party. A Texas congressman who comes to look into the case for statehood has mixed reactions. He hates nonwhites; he knows the rich are the saviors of the republic, but he also hates Republicans. When a labor leader tells him that Hawaii will go Democrat with Shigeo Sakagawa as a state senator, he is, however, appalled. Yet when Shigeo takes him to his home and he learns of Shigeo's part in saving the lost Texas battalion, he gets "a faint glimmer of the ultimate brotherhood in which the world must one day live."

Hoxworth Hale, in spite of his conservative upbringing, perhaps because of his South Sea idyll during the war and because of his awareness of the unity of nature, begins to recognize the unity of mankind. He asks himself concerning alien elements, "What vital thing do they add that keeps our society healthy?" He brings Hong Kong Kee into the establishment as one of the trustees of Malama Kanakoa Estate (she cannot be trusted to handle money). Hong Kong's daughter Judy slips easily into the frieze of Hawaiian ladies, is drawn into their singing, and is even honored with the supreme role in the ritual "Wedding Song." She organizes Kelly's life as singer in nightclubs and on records. To the tourists they are an outstanding professional team, but to the old-time residents of Hawaii this shared enterprise is shocking on traditional racial-solidarity grounds. Malama, however, is all for their marriage: maybe Judy can make Kelly grow up. Hong Kong and the Kees are opposed. To them she would be "a lost girl."

The culminating success story is that of the Saka-gawas. In 1954 Kamejiro and his wife go home to Japan to live. When they venture into Hiroshima, they are forced to recognize that their delusion about a somehow triumphant Japan is ridiculous. What they really discover is that they are no longer comfortable with the old ways—even the toilets, for example—after their life in Hawaii. The intelligent and cultivated wife of Goro also goes home to Japan, because basically both Goro and Shigeo are peasants and life is too short for her to wait for the growing up of a sophisticated community in Hawaii. Surprisingly, Shigeo is helped in his campaign for the territorial senate by Noelani Hale Janders, who says the Republicans are worn-out for the time being: "I've been living a long time with worn-out people, so I'm ready to accept new ideas." Shigeo, invited to join one of the important governing boards, says he will be glad to *after* the election but that he will not give up his drive for land reform. After the election Democrats control both houses for the first time, and the majority of the elected Democrats are Japanese, "the best-educated, most-dedicated group of legislators elected that day" in the United States. Hoxworth Hale brings Shigeo a *maile lei*—which is better than a crown—and publicly invites him to the board of Whipple Oil. A new day has begun.

This novel is impressive above all for its control of vivid pseudo-historical fact concerning four disparate ethnic groups. The reader never doubts the authenticity of what he is reading. He identifies with about equal absorption with all four of the group histories. Whatever his initial prejudices, he has to admit that all four groups were, at least initially, heroic in their effort to establish and achieve reasonable goals. While characterization in depth is never Michener's forte, enough of the characters are so well drawn that they are not speedily forgotten. The Polynesians come off least well in that respect, for obvious reasons. Their way of life offered little in the way of written or artistic evidence as to what they thought and felt. After the legendary figures of the early voyage the most convincing native figure is Kelly Kanakoa, but it is inevitable that some advocates of ancient Polynesian life will look upon him as a caricature. Abner Hale, John Whipple, Rafer Hoxworth, and Jerusha Hale, plus Nyuk Tsin, stand head and shoulders above the rest of the characters. None of the Japanese group is outstanding, unless it be Kamejiro, who shares the heroic stature of the early figures.

As Michener presents the history of Hawaii through four major ethnic groups it is manageable and sufficiently broad. To be sure, the Filipinos and the Portuguese are left out, no doubt to their distress, but in fact their struggles would merely provide repetition. Michener manages historical data with rare finesse. His personalities are almost entirely fictional. Such real people as King Kamehameha, Queen Liliuokalani, and Father Damien must be mentioned, even seen, but their places in the story are incidental. Historical events are inserted with the same tact. Missionaries did come. Whaling vessels did put into port with riotous results. Sugar and pineapples, as well as irrigation to nurture them, were a major activity. There was intrigue at the end of the century to get Hawaii under United States sovereignty. There was plague and fire in the Chinese section of Honolulu. The island Japanese did fight with distinction in Europe. And the culmination of the process of amalgamation and growth was the achievement of statehood to which the novel points. But these events are merely part of the backdrop for the actions and interactions of credible fictional beings.

Any historical novel worth its salt is more than mere chronicle. Overtly or implicitly it extols or condemns— or at least brings into question—a set of values. What is extolled in *Hawaii* is fortitude—heroism, if we wish— hard work, and adaptability to change. Hawaii is a better place than when it was a *tabula rasa* waiting for the imprint of human settlers, all of whom exhibited heroism in getting there and showed dynamic force in modifying their environment. Because of their relatively brief history as a human crossroads these islands have the chance to cradle something new, a genuine multi-racial society.

That is the ideal held up by the novel. The other side of the shining gold piece is the constant danger to human well-being from self-limiting bigotry, be it racial or religious. Michener had touched on this moral ignominy in his earlier novels. Here it engages our full attention. There is remarkably little preaching on the subject in this novel—much less than, later, in *The Covenant*—but the dismal effects of intolerance are clear, even in the reluctant witness of Hoxworth Hale. There are shocking demonstrations of an automatic intolerance in Abner Hale's repeated discovery of "abominations," in Rafer Hoxworth's inhuman treatment of the Chinese on board his ship, in the brutal unconcern for the lepers on Molokai, and by veiled criticism of the way the mainland Japanese were treated after Pearl Harbor. These various demonstrations are, to my mind, emphatic and therefore more memorable than the rainbow annunciation of the Golden Men.

It took nine weeks for *Hawaii* to make it to the top of the best-seller list. Its major successors got there much faster.

3

Two Poles of Mediterranean Culture: *The Source* (1965), *Iberia* (1968)

The origins of Michener's two books on Mediterranean lands are strikingly dissimilar. He tells us that for ten years he had been studying Muslim culture with a view to writing a book about it when, on a visit to Israel, he suddenly conceived a novel dealing with the history of the Jews. The episodes that he jotted down on the spur of the moment became, without change, the content of *The Source*, which he completed in two years. *Iberia*, on the other hand, had a long gestation. Michener fell in love with Spain on a brief visit in 1932. He returned repeatedly to savor its special cultural flavor, and finally published his book in 1968, a labor of love and a testimony of special devotion.

The Source

The Source (1965) is the most ambitious, the most intricate, and undoubtedly the most searching of Michener's novels. It traces Jewish spiritual and cultural identity from its beginnings through the formulation of religious laws, through recurrent persecutions and dispersions, to the establishment of an ambivalent secular state in 1948, with an even more ambivalent forecast of the future. All this in slightly more than nine hundred pages.

The historical narrative (or narratives) is framed by

a contemporary action that permits cross-references to historical events and evaluation of some of them. In 1964, according to the story, an archeological dig of importance, financed by a Chicago Jew named Zodman, is begun at Makor, seven or eight miles from the port of Akko. It is this fictional site, bearing resemblance to actual digs, that serves as the locus for thirteen of the fifteen historical narratives that are the body of the novel. Since Makor is no longer inhabited in the nineteenth and twentieth centuries, the last two episodes take place at Safed, a few miles away, but in both cases significant action also occurs at Makor.

The dig is under tripartite direction, though technically under the leadership of John Cullinane, an Irish-Catholic from the Biblical Museum in Chicago. His adjutants are Dr. Ilan Eliav, a government administrator as well as an archeologist, who ultimately becomes a member of the Israeli cabinet, and Jamil Tabari, who is Oxford trained and one of the few Arabs who remained in Israel when it became a Jewish state in 1948. Another assistant is Dr. Vered Bar-El, one of the first experts to have been trained wholly in Israel. What we learn later is that all three of these people were involved in the fighting between Jews and Arabs at Safed, in passing at Makor, and at Akko. There is a thread of amatory intrigue in that both Cullinane and Eliav want Vered to marry them. Because of religious incompatibilities she refuses both, marrying Zodman and going to live in America. This intrigue is of little importance except as it brings out the rigidity of Jewish law.

The Tell—that is, the mound at Makor to be excavated, which is seventy-one feet above bed rock—is "the patiently accumulated residue of one abandoned settlement after another, each resting upon the ruins of its predecessor, reaching endlessly back into history." It is "the meticulous recreation of that history" which is the task of the novel as well as of the archeological expedition. Two trenches are dug at different points. There is considerable drama as the months go by and artifacts from various periods of history are retrieved, such as a menorah (the seven-branched ritual candelabrum), a statuette of the goddess Astarte, the seal of the Crusader Count Volkmar, a stone from a synagogue reused as a church, a horned altar of King David's time, and coins of various rulers. Fifteen of these objects form links with the fifteen narratives, providing a symbolic referent for each. Other linkage comes from recurrence of or reference to recognizable names from past eras. This is not really necessary but it undoubtedly gives readers some orientation.

Another device is the use of pictorial material. At the beginning of each episode one of the artifacts is reproduced and briefly described. In addition, for nearly every episode there are two maps, one of the region and one a plan of Makor itself at the time in question. The regional maps vary from concentration on Galilee to coverage of the whole eastern Mediterranean. Each gives towns the names current at that particular time. Makor is always Makor, which means "source"; that is, a spring that ensures life in a region where water is rare. (The French Crusaders, by linguistic inadvertence on either their part or the author's, refer to the town as Ma Coeur.) Other names vary. To take only one example, the seaport visible from the walls of Makor is successively Akko, Accho, Ptolemais, St. Jean d'Acre, Akka, Acre— and, in the state of Israel, Akko.

As always in the big Michener novels, precise and overwhelming attention is given to topographical detail. This is the crossroads of the ancient world, where caravans from north, south, and east converge as they seek to trade with ships from the west arriving at Akko. It is also the promised land described by Moses, full of milk and honey. With the passage of centuries the land grows in fruitfulness until in Muslim days come invasions by warriors from the desert, who turn the land back to aridity, leaving only the olive trees. It is not until the Jews return in 1948 that there is a new union between men and land, a new fruitfulness. The returning Jews shake off the stereotype of citydweller and moneylender to till the land. The novel asserts that part of the tragedy of the Middle East is that the Arabs have not remained to share that basic fruitful labor.

The remote situation of Makor enables Michener to avoid the pitfalls involved in using many historical figures. In the Roman era we do in fact come into contact with Herod Antipater, with Josephus, the Jewish general, and with the emperors-to-be Vespasian, Titus, and Trajan—just as, earlier, King David comes briefly on scene in Makor. These appearances are, of course, nonhistorical, but within the terms of the story they are possible. Later on a number of the leading crusaders are vaguely present, as are some of the emperors and sultans who rule in Constantinople. Of later historical figures, however, only Peter the Hermit, of the First Crusade, was really on scene, and that only briefly. For the rest, the personalities are fictional, though the names are often evocative, such as that of Gomer, the prophetess in the fifth episode, a name mentioned in Hosea 1:03.

The novel begins and ends with long sections of the archeological frame story at the dig in 1964. In addition there are interruptions taking the reader back to the present in all but two of the historical episodes. Roughly seventy pages are taken up by these intrusions. The reader wonders if they are really necessary. Sometimes they seem clumsy; sometimes they are obviously expository; on occasion they do serve to establish a parallel between present and past. This novel is, granted, continuously in need of historical explanation. Since this is not always possible through the characters in the frame story, sometimes there is resort to undisguised narrator interruption. One wishes that Michener had done this better or, indeed, had taken a chance and not done it at all.

In the frame story the archeologists number the successive levels of cultural activity from the top down. Thus Level XV is at the beginning of human occupancy of Makor. The narratives, however, proceed from past to present, from the bottom of the dig up; that is, by diminishing numbers. Rather than summarize the action of each of the fifteen historical episodes, which vary in intensity and interest to a considerable degree, I shall pick out and substantiate from the narrative some of the themes that make up the novel and lead, presumably, to a conclusion.

One of the important points made in the opening frame section is that these excavations go to the "foundations of the three great religions," which, as we know, all lay claim to Jerusalem as a holy city and which have all been nurtured by the desert experience of vastness and isolation. (Wisely, Jerusalem is presented only as a goal, an ideal. We are there only briefly in "The Voice of Gomer.") We are made aware of the simple animistic origins of early worship among the lesser tribes, producing practices that the Hebrew newcomers call abominations. We see very little of the origins of Christianity and Mohammedanism. It is rather the zealotry and embattled sectarianism of these faiths that are stressed.

Against such a background two main questions are pursued. The broad one is whether a true ecumenism can exist among these religions, or if the two younger faiths are destined to visit outbreaks of savage intolerance upon the Jews through all time. A narrower question is raised early by John Cullinane: "Why do Jews make things so difficult for themselves... and others?" Both questions come up for discussion among the 1964 representatives of these religions. The historical continuity that causes these questions to arise, or that shows actions in the public arena that exacerbate them, is the

thread that binds the fifteen historical narratives together. What we are shown as far as Jews are concerned
is testimony of heroic endurance almost beyond belief,
balanced against a rigidity of law so austere as on occasion to be antihuman. These two sets of evidence are
not black and white. Each is ambiguous. Within each is
constant need to adjust the balance sheet of gain and
loss. Whether or not the unaffiliated, nonpartisan reader
ever finds a fixed point in his own oscillation of response
is open to question. What is certain is that he has had
an experience of such power as to be almost unique. He
has gone to the well at Makor, which is symbolically
the source of all Middle Eastern and Western history.

The initial ambiguity appears in Level XIII (the
third historical narrative), where desert nomads, the Ha-
biru (forerunners of the Hebrews) come to Makor by
divine command. They respect the gods of the community but quietly insist on the primacy of their mon-
otheistic deity, El-Shaddai, particularly over Baal and
Astarte. To Baal, a god of death, the firstborn son of
every union is consecrated. In palliation of this rite of
death there is the institution of temple-priestess prostitution, and especially a rite by which a man chosen by
the priests is publicly honored to be the first enjoyer of
a new priestess of Astarte, who represents life. So intense
is the experience of even those who only witness this
rite that for a time they are in danger of forgetting El-
Shaddai and of seeking actively to commit abominations.

Perhaps there was a moment when Canaanites and
Hebrews, who "had started their national histories by
sharing the same god, El, who represented unseen
power," had a possible basis of understanding and accommodation. But right from the start they treated their
deity in different ways. The Canaanites diminished his
universal qualities, fragmented him into homely functions, and seemed to "drag him down to their level."

The Hebrews freed him of the local and parochial. "Each modification the Hebrews introduced in the desert years intensified the abstract powers of El." In other words, the Canaanites were degrading the concept of god, while the Hebrews were elevating it.

On the social level, the nomadic, pastoral Hebrews held the view that the ways of the city-dwelling Canaanites were corrupt and corrupting; whereas the Canaanites believed that only when men dwelt in communities was there the possibility of constructive and innovative growth. In this episode such a conflict of values breaks into the open when a granddaughter of Zadek, the Hebrew patriarch, is made pregnant by Zibeon, son of the Canaanite leader. God orders the destruction of the town and the death of every man. The women are to be divided among the conquerors, who will take the children to rear as their own. God makes it clear that he does this not "because I hate the Canaanites, but because I love you." A just man may, however, be spared. Zibeon accepts the one god and through his children makes certain that "the great family of Ur would survive."

The fourth episode, "Psalm of the Hoopoe Bird," takes place in the reign of King David. By this time, "Yahweh, the god of Moses, a new Hebrew deity who had developed step by step from El-Shaddai," is so mighty that he controls both the high heavens and the deep heart of man. In Makor a descendant of Zibeon of the previous episode is accepted as an honest Hebrew and is married to Kerith, the daughter of a priest.

This was the golden morning of Makor, the glorious apex of the town; it was also the period when Hebrews were demonstrating their ability to govern a kingdom, and if Makor were to be taken as the criterion, they governed well.

It is, however, still pretty much a Canaanite town, resisting or ignoring the austerity of Hebrew belief.

The conflict we witness is on a very personal level, for Kerith's husband, Jabaal, affectionately known as "the Hoopoe Bird" for his clumsy, earthy nature, is concerned only with the building of a tunnel for convenient and secure access to the well. Kerith puts up with this nonsense in the hope that his building skill will gain notice and the king will invite him to Jerusalem, the fount of religious feeling. Hoopoe is willing to compromise his religious beliefs when he goes to the seaport to purchase special tools. A good man, he deals with concrete things, in contrast to Gershon, an outlaw, who comes to Makor for sanctuary. Gershon is an inspired singer, a psalmist, "unequivocal where his testimony concerning Yahweh was concerned." He plays and sings for King David when the latter visits the town to inspect the tunnel. We are informed that the king "placed the abstract wisdom of Jerusalem athwart the pragmatic values of Makor," ignoring Hoopoe's accomplishment and frustrating Kerith's hopes. She therefore goes with Gershon to Jerusalem and witnesses King David's remorse over a hot-tempered order he had given to kill a Moabite slave who was Hoopoe's assistant. In time Hoopoe dies. Nothing of his achievement as builder will remain, whereas "the poet, regardless of the expense in human lives, had glimpsed the true face of Yahweh." The nature of the right way is clear and incontrovertible. Or so it seems. But in 1964 Cullinane and his group rediscover the tunnel, which is hailed as "a masterpiece of construction" and of which a French philosopher claims: "this mute genius of the Makor water system speaks to modern man more cogently than those who wrote the Psalms.... His tunnel is a psalm in fact, the song of those who accomplish God's work." And the Hoopoe, Jabaal of Makor, has indeed left his own spiritual legacy. Inscribed on the ceiling of the tunnel is his testamentary cry: "From the heavens Yahweh directed! From the earth Baal. Praise to the gods who sustain us."

The four first historical episodes are a kind of prelude to the suffering and dispersions of the Jews and the parallel development of an intractable, adamantine, detailed set of laws. In Level XI, "The Voice of Gomer," we learn at once that "These were the generations when Yahweh smote his Hebrews, for he still found them a stiff-necked people." To this end he used the Assyrians in 701 B.C., the Babylonians in 612 B.C., and in 609 B.C. the Egyptians, who killed King Josiah at Megiddo. In Makor, much diminished after these invasions, Jeremoth of the family of Ur is content to serve as governor, whatever invader holds power. Rimmon, the son of Gomer, a poor widow, is the superintendent of Jeremoth's olive grove. He is a handsome and marriageable young man, but he and his mother worship Yahweh (Rimmon in fact worships Yahweh for moral guidance and Baal for success in his daily work). Gomer is sure her son has a special destiny, and this is confirmed when on the way to the well Yahweh speaks to her three times in no uncertain terms. She and her son are to journey to Jerusalem for the week of festivals. It is only in Jerusalem that one can see "the solemn passion of an entire people, coming to focus on one splendid temple," the one built by Solomon. Rimmon is much moved by this experience and on the sixth day exclaims:

O Jerusalem, if I forget you let my eyes be blinded, let my right hand lose its cunning.

Mikal, Jeremoth's daughter, participates in the festivals and Rimmon falls in love with her and marries her over his mother's opposition. Gomer comes to cherish her loving and helpful daughter-in-law, even though she has misgivings about her because her family are "more Canaanite than Hebrew." Then the great army of Pharaoh comes up from the south to crush Babylon, requisitioning supplies and two hundred men from Makor, Rimmon among them. Egypt is overwhelmed, most of the men from Makor are blinded and taken into slavery by Nebuchadrezzar. In a spirit of resistance, the citizens of Makor, mostly women, rebuild the walls. Gomer first says that Yahweh will bless Jeremoth for this, but then Yahweh speaks to her once more and tells her the walls must not be finished and that "In chains and yokes shall you march to Babylon. It is the destiny of Israel to perish from the land it has known, that it may find its god once more." Rimmon is released unharmed. Once more Yahweh speaks, telling him that during the punishment in the years ahead Rimmon must remember not Babylon but Jerusalem.

"Guided by a force outside herself," Gomer throws down a stone from the well. She grabs and breaks the governor's staff. She goes to the temple of Astarte and drives out the priestess-prostitutes. For a time she resists Yahweh's command to drive out the daughters of Canaan because of her regard for Mikal, but at last she is forced to assert God's will. She summons the children of Israel to come with her to topple the statue of Baal.

The authorities imprison this confused old woman to keep her out of mischief, but she breaks out and sets fire to the temple of Astarte. Then she is chained at the bottom of the well shaft, from which her superhuman voice can still be heard in prophecy: "All is desolation. Israel is condemned to wander across the face of the earth. You have been faithless. You have been evil." When the city puts up an unexpectedly valiant defense, Yahweh opens a way in for the enemy. Gomer conveys Yahweh's promise that he will be with his beloved children of Israel, "no matter how harsh their exile." "The world shall be yours and the sweetness thereof, for when you accept my punishment you also accept my divine compassion." Gomer prophesies Nebuchadrezzar's defeat by the Persians. He has had enough of her and has her stabbed. Her body is entombed at the entrance to the well, where she had first talked with Yahweh.

The next devastation of uprooting and suffering comes more than five hundred years later, in "Yigal and the Three Generals," when the Jews rise up against the Roman occupation and the abominations of Caligula and Nero. When the army is about to bring a statue of the god Caligula to Makor, the Jews of the city, led by an ordinary man named Yigal, lie down before the Roman legions on the outskirts of Ptolemais. The general is sufficiently impressed to send a message to Rome advising that the Jews be allowed their particular form of worship. Caligula's response, predictably, is to order that the Jews be completely destroyed and that the general commit suicide. The city and the general are saved by the assassination of Caligula.

Thirty years later comes a recurrence of terror under Nero, who orders the destruction of Jerusalem and the leveling of the Temple. This task is entrusted to Vespasian, assisted by Titus and Trajan. As usual, it is tactically necessary to overcome the outpost of Makor. By the spring of 67 A.D. Makor is still holding out, but the Romans have killed twenty thousand Jews in Caesarea and fifty thousand in Alexandria. Yigal repeats his stand of a generation before. When the town is taken, Vespasian orders the crucifixion of Yigal and his wife. The nine hundred remaining Jews are herded together in front of the crosses; most of the males will be executed on the spot, the rest will become slaves. Only a few of the women are found fit for service; the rest are slain in a few minutes. All children under eight are killed; of the older ones only a few are thrown into iron cages for transportation to the slave market at Rhodes. The walls of Makor are torn down and the entire city is burned.

Early in the Byzantine era (Level VII) there is a new subjugation and dispersion. The Jews resist the excessive taxation by their overlords and are unaccommodating to the demands of a new religious environment. An army of Germanic mercenaries is dispatched to Galilee.

They quickly destroy all things Jewish, such as the synagogue in Makor. Father Eusebius, who has become bishop of the area, takes advantage of the opportunity to place the basilica of St. Mary Magdalene on the site of the destroyed synagogue. Rabbi Asher, a mild Jewish leader who has been among those compiling the Talmud in Tiberias for many years, determines that his flock must migrate to Babylonia. Those who refuse to follow him go into exile from the port of Ptolemais. For the fourth time Makor is stripped of its Jews—and, for the first time, from strictly religious motivation.

Such obduracy is repeated with the coming of the Muslims around 635 A.D., as recounted in "A Day in the Life of a Desert Rider." When the Jews of Medina resist Muhammad's overtures and publicly ridicule the Koran, the retaliation is swift. The eight hundred Jews of Medina are led to an open trench in the market place, into which they fall as they are beheaded—all but one, who cannily allows himself to be converted. Muhammad generously marries the widows of two of the leaders he has been forced to execute. Military units fan out over the Middle East. When Abd Umar, a black Muslim (who had been reared by a Jewish merchant, Ben Hadad), comes to Makor, he respects the decision of Jews and Christians to adhere to their own faiths but kills two pagans who do not convert instantly. The descendants of the original Canaanites get the point and shift allegiance readily. Thus the arrival of Islam does not initially disperse the Jews, though in some cases they suffer.

A new crisis comes to Jewry unexpectedly and spontaneously in 1096 as members of the First Crusade set out up the valley of the Rhine. One of the leaders, Gunter, brother of Count Volkmar of Gretz, happens to see a Jew as the mob is shouting "Death to the Infidel." Crusading zeal is directed at the unfortunate Jew and at 1,800 of his brethren before the Crusaders withdraw from Gretz. It is "the beginning of a heritage that would haunt Germany forever." The killings continue as the Crusaders proceed: 30,000 in Germany alone. In all fairness it must be noted that the Crusaders continue to be involved in killings and retaliations all the way to Constantinople. Of the 16,000 Crusaders who started in the valley of the Rhine fewer than 9,000 remain when they reach the Golden Horn in October 1096. Of Gunter's advance force of rabble only seven survive in Asia Minor, where they distinguish themselves by killing robed Christians whom they mistake for Muslim infidels. As we are told by the archeologist, Tabari, "the Crusaders doomed themselves when they failed to establish an alliance with the Arabs," since their real enemies were the Kurds and Turks. Count Volkmar actually has better luck than most. He ensconces himself in Makor, where he dies and is succeeded by seven generations of the same name.

In the following episode, almost two hundred years later, the Crusaders are on the decline and arrange a ten-year truce with the conquering Mamelukes (Asiatic slaves imported by the Turks but who have taken over the Turks' empire). A contingent of peasant pilgrims from northern Italy go berserk at St. Jean d'Acre, killing all and sundry infidels and thus giving an excuse for the breaking of the truce. Makor is taken after a siege and is completely leveled. The well shaft is filled in. By 1450 every sign of human occupancy has been erased: "It was a mound rising from the foothills of the Galilean mountains." Wind continues to blow in from the desert; and the land of milk and honey itself becomes a desert. Occasionally bedouins sweep in, killing such farmers as have returned to try to revive the soil. This is no Jewish homeland.

In Level III we get an account of what might be called the first official and systematic modern persecutions. This episode brings together three saintly men from fictional localities: Rabbi Zaki from the Italian sea-

port of Podi, Dr. Abulafia from the Spanish town of
Avaro, and Rabbi Eliezer bar Zadok, whose ancestors
migrated from Babylonia as groats makers a thousand
years before. Zadok has come recently from Gretz. Earlier, each of these men had felt an initial security, but
in the community of each the forces of persecution and
dehumanization of Jews were on the rise. There was
expulsion from Spain in 1492, vehement denunciation
by Martin Luther a generation later, and vacillating papal
directives in southern Italy. The sufferings of all three
of these men and their families were extreme, though
their countries differed. All three of the men, forced to
flee, arrive eventually in Safed, where they give themselves to rabbinic study.

The last of the historical narratives, "Rebbe Itzik
and the Sabra," recounts the victory of Jewish armed
resistance in 1948, when the British give up their man-
date over Palestine, expecting the Arabs to take over
and any Jew so foolhardy as to remain to be slaughtered.
A modern miracle occurs. Against incredible odds a
Jewish commando force captures Safed. The Arabs are
so disorganized by rumor that they flee without a prolonged fight. Elsewhere the outcome is the same, and
the state of Israel is born. However, the fact that the
Arabs have left permanently makes the victory somehow tarnished. But at least a new conception of Jewish
nature and Jewish moral obligation has come into being:
they will no longer submit to oppression, humiliation,
and torture; there will be no further diasporas.

Thus concludes a tracing of *The Source*'s first main
question: whether a true ecumenism can exist among
the three religions whose holy city is Jerusalem. The
other, second thematic strand—Jewish formulation of
and adherence to a remarkably narrow and inflexible
body of law—is of equal importance. By its insistence
on literal and minute interpretation this body of law
becomes inhuman and destroys individuals. Already in

"The Voice of Gomer" we have an instance of Yahweh-authorized inhumanity when Rimmon is forced to put away his wife, Mikal.

The most dramatic account of inflexibility occurs in Level X, "In the Gymnasium." It is also the most painful, for reasons that will become apparent. Makor is under the rule of Antiochus IV, who in 17 B.C. demands that all citizens of his empire acknowledge him as a god, Antiochus Epiphanes, the embodiment of Zeus. For the time being Jews are allowed the idiosyncrasies of their worship if they pay homage to Antiochus. Two years later there is an order that, in the interest of not perpetuating differences among the subject peoples, Jews shall no longer circumcise their male offspring. The final blow is an order to sacrifice four times a year at the altar of Antiochus Epiphanes, the sacrificial offering to be a swine.

The district governor, named Tarphon, is of Canaanite extraction, is an excellent athlete trained in Athens, and is conciliatory toward the Jews. He protects them as much as possible but thereby causes them to be completely unprepared for the harshness of Antiochus. Tarphon, who has established a gymnasium at Makor, encourages young athletes. Among them is a youth called Menelaus, son of the rabbi Jehubabel. He is so promising a wrestler that Tarphon hopes he will be able to enter the games at Antioch and ultimately those at Athens and even Olympia. But there is a basic culture conflict here. To the Jews, sports are irrelevant and public nudity an affront; to the Greeks, sports and nudity are an assertion of health and beauty. This poses a particular problem for Menelaus, since Antiochus has ordered that no contestant who has been circumcised may stand before him at the games. Tarphon tells Menelaus that in Ptolemais there is a physician who "can cover the sign"; that is, repair the circumcised penis. Menelaus undergoes the ordeal and in time is ready to compete at Makor against

the visiting wrestlers from Cyprus. He and the other
athletes march naked into the gymnasium. The Jewish
community, who have been forced to attend, avert their
eyes from the indecent sight until they hear shouts of
praise that Menelaus is now "one of us." His father's
eyes are affronted by the change in his son: "And the
uncircumcised man child whose flesh of his foreskin is
not circumcised, that soul shall be cut off from his people; he hath broken my covenant." In wrath the father
rises and smites his son, whom he calls Benjamin, unto
death. In an interpolated Tell commentary just before
this dramatic event Eliav wishes the Jews had learned
the discipline of sports and rejoices that they are com-
peting at last in the Olympic Games, that they are dis-
covering "that in these matters the Greeks were right."

Another emphatic instance of the harshness of the
law comes in Level VII, entitled "The Law," which
describes the ways of Jewry in the early days of the
Byzantine Empire. Christianity has been decreed the
official religion in 313 A.D. In 326 Constantine's mother,
St. Helena-to-be, after disembarking at Ptolemais, had
come to Makor and had a vision directing the building
of a basilica to St. Mary Magdalene in that town. The
altar was to be placed precisely on that spot where in
millennia gone by other religions had celebrated their
rites. In these early years of Christian growth, God was
"at the same time perfecting His first religion, Judaism,
so that it might stand as the permanent norm against
which to judge all others." Part of that perfecting was
the setting down and codifying of ancient traditional
law. Rabbi Asher of Makor is caught up in that work,
spurred on by accounts of legendary rabbis like Akiba,
who had begun the work. Now in the fourth century
A.D. a group of devoted rabbis spend all their time in
Tiberias on the Sea of Galilee, analyzing and debating
the law.

There is considerable description (for most readers

too much) of the "patient, involuted and often arbitrary manner [by which] the great rabbis wove that net in which God would hold his chosen people." More important for the novel is the net in which two of the fictional characters are caught. Yohanon, a stonecutter, wishes to marry Tirza, whose husband has vanished and must be presumed dead. Rabbi Asher says fifteen years must pass. Yohanon marries in spite of such a ruling. The child Menahem is therefore a bastard; he can never marry or participate in Jewish religious life. No bar mitzvah is possible for him. Jewish girls may not consort with him, since marriage within the faith will not be allowed him.

According to Jewish law there is only a devious way out of this impasse. If Menahem steals an object worth more than ten drachmas, is tried and convicted and then sold into slavery to a Hebrew family, after five years he can marry another Hebrew slave and become free. Their children will be welcomed into the Jewish faith, but even then the parents will not be. This is not an attractive course of action, though Menahem does consider it. When Father Eusebius tells him that "the church of Jesus Christ is available without restraint," both father and son are baptized, and the weight of the old law is dissolved in the freedom of the new. Menahem, now called Mark, is, however, immediately confused by the conflicting doctrines within the Christian church—a conflict that will demoralize Christianity for centuries. As mentioned earlier, Father Eusebius drives the Jews out of Makor for the fourth time. The basilica occupies part of the site of the destroyed synagogue. Yohanon, now called John, works on it, but without the joy of his earlier craftsmanship. Mark disappears into the Syrian desert, "from which he would emerge years later a theologian of great power."

As the reader proceeds through the novel he encounters many instances of the dehumanizing pressure of the law. In Level VI, a woman raped by her brother-in-law gets no help because she is too ashamed to report the assault at once. When the brother-in-law kills her husband she is obliged by the law to become that man's wife. In Level II, Schmuel Hacohn, son of a Russian rabbi who was killed in a pogrom, comes to Galilee with money entrusted to him to buy land for a colony. Not only is he the victim of administrative bad faith on the part of the Turkish government, but he is turned upon by the Jewish community and tried on charges of not observing the laws strictly and not studying in the synagogue. He is to be fined to the amount of his possessions, then stripped, stoned, and banished from Palestine. In Level I, with war for an independent Israel imminent, Rabbi Itzik holds to the old ways, in which the goal for Jewish men is to sit day after day in study of the Torah. This is what one of the new-breed partisans calls "so much Mickey Mouse crap."

The culmination of this narrow legalism comes in the final frame chapter, where we see the well-being of many individuals, including Vered and Eliav, blocked by the law. Though her husband was a hero who died in the 1948 war, Vered may not marry Eliav because the law demands that she marry her deceased husband's brother. By a perverse twist of legalism that brother, resident in Turkey, is so fed up with legalisms that he has refused to acknowledge their existence, and therefore will not sign papers to release Vered.

Eliav himself in his new cabinet post will be the arbiter and interpreter of the law in a delicate attempt to achieve a balance between insistence on the old and the need for the new. Three cases are cited. Trudi Ginzberg, a gentile from Gretz, married a Jew, protected him from the Nazis, and eventually brought him to Israel. Parallel to the judgment on Yohanon in "The Law," more than fifteen hundred years before, the judgment is that she and her children can never be accepted as

Jews. In the second case, two natives of India, whose Jewishness goes back four hundred and fifty years, cannot be accepted on the ground that there is no record of their adherence to the faith. Thus they cannot marry in Israel. They are religious outcasts. Finally there is the case of the Jew from Brooklyn who after a successful career as hotelier wants to build a grand hotel in Akko. He will abide strictly by dietary laws, but the rabbis find all sorts of objections to his project on other grounds, such as having no fire on the Sabbath, which they interpret as meaning no turning of an electric switch, since that might cause a spark to flare. When they insist that even the automatic doors between kitchen and dining room may not operate on the Sabbath, the would-be entrepreneur gives up, saying: "You're making it too complicated to be a Jew."

In this analysis of *The Source* only a few salient instances of Jewish suffering and of Jewish rigid adherence to the law have been cited. These two themes are the substance of the work, which abounds in comments about the dilemma created:

Judaism was a hard, tough old religion that didn't give the individual enough free play. It could never have appealed to the world at large.

When Christianity came in with its promise of a new dispensation, Judaism moved backward and became harder. But

if it was true that he [Rabbi Asher from Gretz] had forged chains of bondage, it was also true that he had built those sturdy bridges on which Jews marched from the past to the present and on into the future.

In the course of the novel we glimpse the sectarian disputes among Christians that have fragmented their religious unity and have fomented genocidal war among them as well as against Jews and pagans. There are in-

timations in the last section that Muslim religion is in
danger of similar sectarian bigotry (verified in the 1980s
in Iran and elsewhere). And in newborn Israel there are
disquieting animosities between the Ashkenazim immigrants from Europe and the Sephardim from North
Africa. So far as I can see, the novel makes no claim
that adamantine interpretation of the law must continue
in order to ensure the continued existence of the Jews.
What it clearly does underwrite is an active, embattled
Jewish community determined to fight for the right to
live, no longer willing to lie down in the belief that if
they suffer enough God will reward them. In short, *The
Source* celebrates Jewish endurance as a coherent identity,
recognizes that this would not have been possible through
centuries of catastrophe without incredible coherence of
faith, but does not necessarily assert that past practice is
the way to new ends.

The tone of this work so far as Jewish–Arab relations are concerned is too optimistic. Three major wars
have occurred in that region since 1965. Unbridled violence has become an end in itself in the once-fertile
crescent. The goal no doubt continues to be what reasonable men have always sought, that the two warring
lions lie down together in peace. But the way is not
clear, the chances of such a solution become increasingly
remote. The novel offers no solution, nor is its purpose
to do so.

Given the importance of this problem, however, we
must touch briefly on some of Michener's comments
on that subject since 1965. In 1970 he published a long
and informed article, "What to Do About the Palestinian
Refugees?" in the *New York Times Magazine*, September
27, 1970. He asserted that after twenty-two years of
turmoil the reason for the Arabs' departure was unimportant. It was the fact of their rotting in camps that
was now the issue. He found the question of who has

a right to Palestine, who owns it, completely irrelevant if not idiotic. "Neither side has owned it by unbroken right of inheritance." He was impatient when he heard Jews say it was "never an Arab land," when it obviously was for more than a millennium. At the same time he felt that the PLO should be outlawed. Their manic violence merely impeded and imperiled a reasoned settlement.

In 1973 Michener was the editor of *First Fruits: A Harvest of 25 Years of Israeli Writing*, celebrating the first quarter of a century of Israel's existence as a new state. In his introduction he recalled the Negev desert in the spring of 1964, seeing after a March rain the desert burst into bloom,

an explosion of color and vitality, a miracle of rejuvenation. Seeds long dormant had been waiting a generation for this rain. . . . Then and now I think of Israel in those terms. It was a land long dormant which sprang to abundant life. Mysteriously it was summoned back to life.

He had, he said, no feeling that Judaism was superior to Christianity or Islam as a religion. Satisfactory societies could no doubt be worked out under the aegis of any of them. But he did admire the spiritual regeneration that accompanied the rebirth of Israel and the way in which it had brought forth new forms of social and intellectual life. This keyed in with the novel, which, in the last analysis, is a song of admiration for a way of life that has endured, even when beaten into the earth, one that has not wavered in its conviction that it is indeed directed by the will and consciousness of God.

Iberia

Michener first saw Spain in the spring of 1932 from the deck of a freighter out of Glasgow as it rounded Cape Finisterre on the Atlantic. He did not step on Spanish

soil until many days later, when he landed at the primitive port of Burriana on the Mediterranean. From there
he saw the urbanity of Spain in Valencia, and on a trip
to Teruel the bitter poverty of those close to the soil.
Since that visit he has regarded Spain as a second home,
responding to it with an intensity equal to that of his
response to Japan. On his repeated visits he became an
aficionado of Spanish character, Spanish art, and Spanish
bullfighting. He became puzzled by the subsidence of
Spain from world power to social anachronism. In 1968
these and other interests converged in *Iberia*, which by
general consent is one of the best books on Spain in this
century and, in the opinion of many, the most interesting book Michener ever wrote.

What he wished to show was "the immemorial aspect of Spain," not the famous touristic things that
everybody writes about. On that very first trip he rode
to shore with a stevedore who looked like a satyr and
had breakfast with him and other laborers in a dockside
café. Since that happy initiation he has made it his business to talk to everybody. And with the collaboration
of the photographer Robert Vavra he studded his book
with pictures of immemorial Spanish faces, worn down
but not subservient, conveying a dignity and independence that defy constraining circumstances.

In organization *Iberia* is anecdotal rather than chron-
ological or analytical. We are alongside Michener in his
excursions, conversations, and meditations, at various
times up through a prolonged visit in 1966, when he
was actually preparing the book. Of the thirteen chapters, ten bear the names of cities, though these are by
no means exclusively about these cities. Such focusing
gives the reader who has a feeling for maps a chance to
know where he is geographically and therefore to some
extent historically. To that end each chapter is preceded
by a map of the region with the chief points of interest
indicated on it. It should be noted at the outset that the

cities so emphasized are, with two exceptions, in the western part of Spain. Of the two exceptions, Teruel comes late in the book and is part of a closing framework; Barcelona, of separate, and separatist, richness of culture, is not quite Spanish and is almost an inescapable addendum, or perhaps a point of reference from which to get bearings on Spain proper.

What does Michener leave out? Predictably and properly the various vacation coasts. He ignores the Costa Brava between the French border and Barcelona. He takes one look at the high-rise forest that appeared in the 1960s north of Alicante and deplores it. As for the Costa del Sol—the stretch of coast on either side of Málaga in the southwest—he cops out on that too. He quotes an acquaintance who describes Torremolinos as

the living most . . . the capital de gustibus . . . the new wave . . . the perpetual party. It's Sweden-on-the-sand. It's the Lourdes of LSD. It's the only spot in Spain where the Guardia Civil doesn't run things.

(When I last saw Torremolinos in 1975, that description scarcely held. The town was overrun by members of the National Retired Teachers Association, and the highway police were as offensive as the Guardia Civil.) Actually, in his novel *The Drifters* Michener has an eighty-page section that depicts the life of the young in Torremolinos during the late 1960s, "when the only people not on a trip [were] the tourists."

There are some omissions that cause surprise, or that at least should be noted. Segovia, just across the Guadarrama range north of Madrid, and Soria (with Numantia recalling the Masada of the Jews), are not even mentioned. Zaragoza and Burgos are mentioned only in passing. Bilbao, the industrial center of the new Spain, does not come under observation, and there is only casual recognition of the unique identity of the Basques. These omissions are not grounds for condemnation. Not all facets of a country must be encompassed by any writer. He has the right to pick and choose so long as he does not distort the picture. Above all, *Iberia* is not a travel guide, though it is a record of travel. It seeks to present a culture that stands out distinctly from the rest of Europe:

For just as this forbidding peninsula physically juts into the Atlantic and stands isolated, so philosophically the concept of Spain intrudes into the imagination in unique ways.

Michener raises questions, which he calls "speculations," as to why Spain is different, why a nation once oriented toward Europe withdrew to semi-isolation, why a dominant world power became a kind of shadow of itself, why government and social privilege in Spain have not over the centuries matured into something beyond the feudal pattern. Such questions as these arise spontaneously as the author leads us through the landscape and the history of this country. Ultimately the answers that he offers must be considered.

The first three cities that we visit, Badajoz, Toledo, and Córdoba, provide three windows to the Spanish past. It is the forbidding landscape which first struck Michener that accounts for his initial emphasis on Extremadura and "the nothing city" of Badajoz. It was from bleak and poverty-sticken Extremadura that so many of the conquistadores set out for the New World, with nothing to lose but their lives. They brought or sent back enormous treasure, little of which remained in their native region, though in Trujillo are remnants of the palaces the Pizarro family built. Thirty years after his first visit to Spain, Michener found in Extremaduran villages a poverty as grinding and undermining as that he had first encountered in the mountains near Teruel.

Badajoz is, as he says, a city without distinction, but it was a major center in Roman Spain after the Second Punic War, when even bleak Extremadura was

important to Roman ascendancy. In due time veterans'
colonies were created there, the most important being
the as yet scarcely excavated Italica near Sevilla, established by Scipio Africanus. Mérida, north of Badajoz,
was the headquarters of a Roman legion. It still has a
Roman bridge that resounded to the feet of soldiers of
the empire as they crossed the Guadiana. One of the
best Roman theaters is preserved there, as well as other
relics of Roman occupation. Badajoz has always been a
fortress city, poised on the Spanish-Portuguese border,
glaring as it were at fortress Elvas on the other side. In
the civil war it was one of the first cities to fall to the
Franco forces, who had their first test of mettle there—
and failed. Some eighteen hundred people were rounded
up by the Franco forces and corraled in the bullring, of
whom probably more than four hundred were machine-
gunned.

If Badajoz and its region remind us of Roman
origins, Toledo, the focus of the following chapter, leads
us back to the time of the Visigoth invaders, who ruled
Spain between Roman days and the time of the Moors
(who came up from Africa in 711). An incomparable
fortress city with the Tagus River as a moat, it is dominated by the soaring tower of the great cathedral and
the arrogant square bulk of the Alcázar—the heroic defense of which is one of the legends of the civil war.
Toledo is the spiritual capital of Spain to this day, but
it makes one think of the medieval church militant, of
the rude strength of faith in the chain mail of unques-
tioning belief. There was a massacre of Jews in Toledo
eighty-seven years before they were expelled from all
of Spain. In the civil war the Republican there went
berserk and threw their victims over the cliff, as had
been done in 1405, proving that "history in Spain has
an ominous way of repeating itself."

Toledo is the city of El Greco, who painted and
left there an abundant spiritual heritage. In his painting

we get the measure of one part of Spanish character.
Goya shows the other part, but Goya does not belong
to Toledo. El Greco's painting,

with its tortured figures and demonic faces, recalls the agonies
which Spain has always inflicted upon itself, the self-condem-
nation, the religious fervor, the leaping of inspired minds directly to the throne of heaven, the impassioned singing and
violence.

In Goya, on the other hand, there is "the earthiness of
Spain, the robust animal-like characteristic of the soil
and the men who work it."

For the Muslim past of Spain Michener chose Córdoba over Granada because the former was "more prosaic and therefore showed the Islamic heritage with less
hyperbole." At its height Córdoba was a city of about
a million inhabitants with three thousand mosques, baths,
and palaces. It was the intellectual center of Islam, not
merely Arab but embracing all the elements of Islamic
culture. The important monument of Córdoba's brilliant past is the great mosque, the Mesquita, built over
the remains of a Visigothic church and in its turn having
a Christian cathedral hewed out of its forest of columns.
The psychological distance between this mosque and the
cathedral in Toledo, Michener writes, "is at least as great
as the distance between the moon and the earth." Five
hundred years after the expulsion of the Moors there
continues to be heated difference of opinion as to their
contribution to Spanish life and character. Michener cites
learned opinion for and against and leaves it at that. But
surely one of the reasons Spain is different is the pressure
of the Muslim presence for half a millennium and the
embattled effort to push it out.

These three cities provide a kind of spectrum of the
origins of Spanish culture; they raise central questions
about the character of the Spanish nation; and they present initially a number of leading figures in history whose

names come up again and again. Nowhere in the volume, I think, is there a fully developed biographical sketch. Rather Michener puts his important personalities together bit by bit, with the result that they become familiar to the reader and central to his understanding. Of these figures the most important are Ferdinand and Isabella, their grandson Charles V of the Holy Roman Empire, their great-grandson Philip II, not to mention pathetic Charles II, the last of the Hapsburg kings of Spain. At a later date come the notorious Ferdinand VII and the lubricious Isabella II, and finally the abdicated Alfonso XIII. Going back to the first Isabella's time, there are Columbus and Cardinal Jiménez de Cisneros; a little later, Ignacio de Loyola, the founder of the Jesuit order, and Velázquez, the great painter-chronicler of royalty. St. Teresa of Avila gets less attention than one would expect. In modern times the chief figures are Sir John Moore, the English general who died fighting Napoleon's army in Spain; José Antonio, the bully-boy saint of Spanish Falangism, who had a street named after him in every city of Spain; and finally General Francisco Franco himself. The names of many bullfighters appear and reappear, including John Fulton of Philadelphia, the first American to find success in the ring. Also there is the ghost of Ernest Hemingway, summoned up by the ubiquitous presence of Kenneth Vanderford, who is almost Hemingway's double. Far in the background of all these are the legendary figures of Santiago de Compostela, El Cid Campeador, and Roland and Charlemagne at the Pass of Roncesvalles.

After the first three cities Michener switches unexpectedly from the continuum of history to something out of time in a way, something permanent and unchanging—up to the present at least. "Las Marismas," as the next chapter is entitled, is a tidal marsh or swampland where the Guadalquivir River makes its way to the Atlantic. It covers an area of less than a thousand square miles, or six hundred thousand acres, of which half is true swampland, the rest free of water most of the year. What drew Michener there was that it is the home of the Concha y Sierra bulls and also one of the world's great bird sanctuaries at a time when encroaching urbanization is making it increasingly hard for birds to exist. It is in this chapter that we get a detailed view of a part of Spain that Michener likens to "a drying oxhide outside the southern door of Europe proper." He sees Spain as "a kaleidescope of high sun-baked plateaus, snow-crowned mountains and swamps of the Guadalquivir." But though he dwells surprisingly briefly on the sweeping plains of Castille and Aragon or on the high Pyrenees and the sudden sierras that dot the south of Spain, he describes the appearance and activity of Las Marismas in loving detail for all four seasons.

The southern part of this area, called the Coto Doñana, was for many centuries set aside as a hunting preserve. For the convenience of hunters a great palace was built in the middle of nowhere out of stone brought as ballast from England in ships that were to carry sherry home. About a century ago this region became the goal of naturalists who wanted to study birds that migrated to the north. The *coto*, which unfortunately is only a small part of the Marismas area, is under the control of the World Wildlife Fund—and just in time, for there is danger that ambitious developers will drain the swamps for agriculture and that the migrant visitors will have insufficient breeding grounds for survival. Michener asserts that Spain has abused her land more than other countries. For five hundred years, as the Moorish hegemony declined and finally ceased, once-fertile areas were destroyed by the great flocks of sheep which, as the result of seigneurial privilege, were allowed to roam unrestricted by fences. There is a peculiar Spanish contempt for those who work with their hands, especially on the soil, but gentlemen may own sheep, though they never see them. This contempt has so far preserved Las Marismas, which, the author prays, will continue to be available "for those to whom ecology is at least as sacred as eschatology."

The next five sections of the book—headed by the names Sevilla, Madrid, Salamanca, Pamplona, and Barcelona—take the reader to centers of contemporary as well as historical Spanish life. Each of these cities has its architectural treasures and its ancient rites, but each is emerging, willy nilly, into the twentieth century. In each section there are descriptions of storied towns in the area: Jerez de la Frontera, south of Sevilla; Alcalá de Henares, where the first great university was founded by Cardinal Cisneros, east of Madrid; out of Salamanca, Madrigal de las Altas Torres, the loveliest name in all of Spain; not far from Pamplona, the pass of Roncesvalles; and the crowning glory of Catalonia at Montserrat.

Each of the title cities has its unique treasure or ritual that Michener describes in loving detail—loving, because he always gets involved in what he is describing. Often the involvement is through the guidance of friends, as in Sevilla, where he sees an acquaintance, a run-of-the-mill businessman, spiritually uplifted by carrying a heavy cross and dragging chains when his confraternity marches one night in Holy Week. Michener's description of the entire Holy Week observance is the best I have ever read, because of an almost involuntary identification without sentimentality or nauseous religious unction. In Madrid he feels close to the nineteenth-century Puerta del Sol and the sixteenth-century anguish of the auto-da-fé in the Plaza Mayor. Above all in Madrid it is the Prado, a Hapsburg family museum, that evokes jubilation, especially over the rich hoard of Velázquez paintings.

Salamanca evokes melancholy: regret for a great university that lost its way and for perhaps the greatest square in Europe, the Plaza Mayor, that has had to yield to parking and the roar of traffic. There is recollection also of two great martyrs in the cause of truth. One, Fray Luis de León, was imprisoned in the late sixteenth century for having translated the Song of Songs into Spanish. After five years he was released, only to be handed over again to the Inquisition. The other martyr was the philosopher and rector of the university, Miguel de Unamuno. On El Día de la Raza, October 12, 1936, Unamuno heard a Franco adherent, the leader of the Spanish Foreign Legion, announce to the Salamanca university that all bookish inclination "would be cauterized with a flaming sword." Unamuno refused to remain tactfully silent, challenging him with the reply "Long live intelligence," and thus defending one of the permanent values of Spain at the risk of his own life.

Pamplona, as the reader knows in advance, garners popularity from the running bulls at the famous San Fermín festival in early July. Michener himself, though recuperating from a severe heart attack, participated in 1966, in the last day's run. It was on that occasion that he saw again and met for the first time two of the bullfighters whom he had watched at Valencia in 1932. What he and multitudes of aficionados at San Fermín felt was that they were "lineal descendants of Ernest Hemingway and his fictional characters who four decades ago [in *The Sun Also Rises*] discovered the high hilarity of San Fermín, which through the years has not diminished." Indeed, Michener came back to this scene for some eighty pages in *The Drifters*, where the youthful dissidents were exposed to a purer experience than the rites of LSD.

It was not until the 1960s that Michener went to Barcelona for the first time and perceived its otherness from the rest of Spain. He responded to the teeming life of the great promenade of Las Ramblas, leading from the Plaza de Cataluña down to the Columbus monument at the harbor. He was fascinated equally by the architectural extravagance of the Gaudí church, La Sagrada Familia, and the excavations beneath the older part of the city of extensive Roman ruins. Chiefly he discerned that Barcelona is an exhilarating intellectual capital. Its inhabitants by their centuries-old orientation toward French culture have a more European outlook than other Spaniards. These Spaniards are the Bostonians of Spain: they read. Publishing is centered there. There is a ferment of ideas among students at the university and among the younger clergy. Madrid fears and attempts to dampen such intellectual ardor.

The last three chapters of *Iberia* have varying functions. Because of his enthusiasm over bullfighting, Michener devotes a whole chapter to "The Bulls." It adds little to what we already know. The calling of the roll of the great bullfighters leaves the non-enthusiast cold. There is, or seems to be, according to Michener, a greater personal aura to the bullfighter in Spain than there is to the football, basketball, or baseball player in this country, but even in Spain the great names like Manolete or the picturesque ones like El Cordobés are no longer widely resonant. Today it is football (soccer) and basketball that set the Spaniard wild.

As indicated earlier, *Iberia*'s Teruel chapter is part of the book's closing frame, begun by Michener's trip to that city in 1932. It is the chapter on Santiago de Compostela, however, that gives unexpected tonality to that frame. It is only incidental to his visit to Santiago that Michener goes one day out to Bayona on the coast and from an elevation views the wide sweep of the Atlantic as it beats upon Cape Finisterre and the whole stretch of Portuguese and Spanish coast—what he had seen more than thirty years before from the deck of a freighter. Many themes of the book converge in this remote western region. It is there that the army of dead Sir John Moore experienced its "Dunkirk" and heroic embarkation at the port of La Coruña. It is from that port and from Vigo that desperate Spanish emigrants fled from poverty to the New World. Not far away is Franco's native town, now called El Ferrol del Caudillo, with epic pretensions that will soon subside beside the enduring fame of Santiago de Compostela.

For the last thousand years pilgrims have converged from all over Europe at that cathedral shrine. Only Rome and Jerusalem have equaled Santiago in importance, and it looms larger than they in symbol and legend, with the cockle shell of Santiago—or St. Jacques or James, as he is known in France and England—and the whole body of French *chansons de geste* composed to entice pilgrims to spend the night in monasteries along the way. Santiago is also the site of Michener's most unexpected testimonial. After his heart attack he had run with the bulls at Pamplona; he had returned to Teruel, where in thought and feeling he "had lived and died with the Spanish Republic"; and now at the great high mass in the cathedral at Santiago de Compostela he had slipped behind the altar, where

I hid in the darkness as if an interloper with no proper role in the ceremonial except that I had completed my vow of pilgrimage and stood at last with my arm about the stone-cold shoulder of Santiago [Matamoros], my patron saint and Spain's.

A most un-Quakerly posture and enthusiasm!

So far we have dipped briefly into the treasury of Spanish culture: architecture, painting, sculpture, music, religious ceremony, and bullfighting. But what has the book to say about the pageant of history and some of its chapters? On the whole, Michener's incremental treatment works well. In spite of apparently casual handling, Spanish history is not merely a thing of shreds and patches and picturesque anecdote. It coheres—a coherence that is aided, to be sure, by dynastic charts and chronologies.

The apogee of Spanish wealth and greatness came

in the sixteenth century. Thereafter there was uninterrupted decline. In Michener's opinion, Isabella's reign was the best Spain would know: "Militarily, financially and spiritually she left Spain a bulwark among the nations." Propaganda that took on the force of legend turned Philip II, her great-grandson, into a diabolic figure in lands outside the Spanish sphere who provided an impetus for Protestant England and the Netherlands to strike back at their feared enemy. Only recently has some justice been done to Philip, some recognition given to his zealous if bureaucratic effort to govern well. The one legitimate charge that should be made against him has not generally been made: he and his father permitted Spanish economic vitality to be sapped; the great infusion of silver and gold from the New World was highly inflationary, and instead of putting this capital to work for the increase of goods, the monarchs diverted it to the Hapsburg Empire, to the adornment and enrichment of the Church, and to ill-conceived military enterprises such as the Spanish Armada in 1588.

Historians have tried to assess the force of the Inquisition and the concomitant expulsion of Muslim and Jewish populations in producing the decline of Spain. No doubt Spain would have been better off agriculturally and commercially if they had remained. The expulsions were not necessarily the work of the Inquisition; they came perhaps from a deep-seated aversion on the part of the people at large to non-Christian elements. Here again legend fed by invective and intemperate response in England and elsewhere makes it difficult to pass judgment. The Inquisition was in full force when Spain was at the height of her power and brilliance in the sixteenth century. However, it did not originate in Spain and was less harsh there than elsewhere. Nevertheless, it continued much longer in Spain and must be seen as a prime agent of Spanish insularity and stunted growth. There was a public burning as late as 1781.

Michener contends that the Spanish found "in this bizarre social weapon a ritual that satisfied some deep national appetite." By its persistence, at any rate, the Inquisition encouraged a closed society, "a mania for homogeneity." As time went on, Spain witnessed an intellectual repression of great magnitude. In 1770 Descartes, Hobbes, and Locke, seminal philosophers of the age, were banned at the University of Salamanca. Michener thinks that the passion for homogeneity, begun by the expulsion of the Moors and Jews and continued by ignorant parochial arrogance—"the joyous provincialism of Spanish thought"—made inevitable the decline of Spain. "An oyster can live to itself, but without grains of sand for agitation it cannot produce pearls."

When *Iberia* was published, Spain had enjoyed more than twenty-five years of peace—to echo the Franco slogan for the celebrations held in April 1964. In spite of some healing of wounds the Spanish are still reluctant to talk about the civil war, and Michener has surprisingly little to say about it, though we know that his sympathy was with the overwhelmed Republic. He ponders the motives that kept him from joining the International Brigade in 1936 and concludes that he was put off by the hysteria of those who flocked to the support of the Republic, and he quickly became dubious about Communist influence and intentions. If he had gone to Spain, he would have come home disillusioned, as John Dos Passos did. In retrospect, it is his conclusion that the brutalities of the two armies were about equal.

Throughout *Iberia* there is repeated uneasiness about what will happen when Franco dies, a speculation in which all Spaniards anxiously engaged. Michener hoped for a quiet transition but was by no means sure it would happen. Oddly, and for no adequate reason, he emphatically preferred the claims of Don Juan, Alfonso XIII's son, to those of Juan Carlos, designated by Franco

as his successor and who, so far at least, has demonstrated that he was an admirable choice.

What is the overall impact of this volume? A spon-
taneous enthusiasm for the landscape, for the dignity
and integrity of individuals, and for the overwhelming
power of Roman, Moorish, and Christian art. Michener
is receptive to folk manifestations, whether they be the
rituals of Holy Week, flamenco music and dancing, or
bullfighting. He admits that the overwhelming flood of
tourists on which Spain now depends for sustenance,
and which by example encourages mediocrity of thought
and values, makes him gag. Assimilation of Spain to the
international banality of the late twentieth century is
clearly something he does not want to see. He averts
his eyes and hopes it will not come to pass. In any event,
Iberia is strongly evocative of a Spain that rests on past
glories. It is a song of high towers that long ago began
to crumble.

4

New Life in New Lands: *Centennial* (1974), *Chesapeake* (1978), *The Covenant* (1980)

With *Centennial* (1974) and *Chesapeake* (1978) Michener was for the first time on known and native ground, or almost. And even at such a late date in his career he did not stay there, for *The Covenant* (1980) took him again to a far place and a spiritually alien setting. Nonetheless these three novels have in common an examination of new beginnings on socially virgin soil.

In his early days in Colorado, 1936 to 1939, Michener says he had come to see "the world and man's relation to it as the basic building block of fiction." He employs such a concept in all three of these novels. He recognized too that the dream of "the Great American Novel" was impossible and wisely settled for less, a mighty microcosm of American life that would perhaps sum up or be indicative of the total experience. Like *Hawaii* the two American novels would cover many generations of social experiment, would faithfully set forth the scheme of things entire, in its sordidness and in its grandeur. *The Covenant* as a parallel effort would achieve something of the same goal, though it appears to be primarily a novel with a social purpose.

Centennial

Michener's three-year residence in Greeley, Colorado, generated an excitement that after many years brought forth this novel. He experienced nature on a grander scale than he had elsewhere. He became physically aware of the overwhelming forces against which men and animals tested their mettle and their fortitude. A sense of the tenuous maintenance of civil order under conditions of primal indifference and primal greed as they had existed on the frontier enlarged his understanding and compassion. Four decades later all this background helped Michener to celebrate part of the American experience in a personal bicentennial tribute.

We have more information about the writing of this novel than we do about any of his others. Not long after its publication Random House brought out *About Centennial: Some Notes on the Novel*, in which Michener explained its genesis and purpose. The book contains stunning and still-unfaded photographs that Michener took during his years in Greeley; they are evidence of his deep love of the area. He tells us that, while there, he came to know Floyd Merrill, a newspaper man knowledgeable about the American tradition. The two made many expeditions out of Greeley. From Merrill's ecological teaching Michener came to comprehend "the meaning of the west and the natural interrelationships that controlled it." That interrelationship is one of the two dominant themes of the novel. The other is the epic settlement of the West—a central example of the making of America and therefore a vehicle for assessing the spiritual condition of the country.

As we have seen already, Michener immerses himself completely in the book he is writing. In part it is this intensity that ensures validity. However, in recent years as a public figure he has found it difficult to maintain such mental and emotional isolation. There were three interruptions in the writing of *Centennial*. In 1970, just after he had decided to embark on the novel, the events at Kent State University diverted his attention for the next nine months or so. Then, in 1972, at the urging of some Pennsylvania clergymen, he undertook a trip to Northern Ireland to see what he could make of that imbroglio. He returned "saddened and perplexed," glad enough, no doubt, to reimmerse himself in the American past, which he understood. Finally, as the novel was nearing completion, the behavior of the top Nixon officials so shamed him that he dropped everything for two weeks to do "Is America Burning?" for the *New York Times Magazine*, "the most difficult piece of writing I have ever engaged in, and perhaps the most important."[1] It must be observed that since anxiety about the state of the nation was a basic concern in the writing of the novel, the Watergate scandals were by no means irrelevant.

Exceptionally in this instance, Michener had considerable help from John Kings, a Britisher turned rancher in Wyoming, who with a British-born photographer then resident in Denver traveled some 25,000 miles with Michener or for him in verification of topographical detail. Even though the author had himself traversed the Oregon Trail several times by car, he wanted his assistants to do it again in order to have independent verification of the accuracy of the fictional journey of Levi and Elly Zendt from Lampeter, Pennsylvania, to Colorado in 1844. According to Kings, there is no landscape in *Centennial* that Michener did not construct from recent scrutiny: "Even his dinosaurs wallow in ponds he personally selected for their use."[2]

As with the other major novels, we can take factual accuracy for granted and proceed to evaluate this novel as artifact and vehicle for the examination of social and moral values. Here Michener again uses the basic structure he had devised for *The Source*. He sets up a contemporary narrative framework to contain twelve chapters of prehistoric speculation and historical narrative that lead up to the present. The identified narrator in the opening and closing chapters is Dr. Lewis Vernor, professor of history at a small collage in Georgia, who is commissioned by a national magazine to examine the salient facts of Colorado history and to write essay accounts of that history. It developes that this is a somewhat demeaning job since the magazine articles are already written and merely await Vernor's independent validation. He takes the job, however, since it is relevant to his next research project, brings prestige to his college, and is very well paid. The reader may feel that this is a rather silly and superfluous device, but it has some utility in that Vernor's editorial comments and his notes at the end of each chapter (patterned after Edward Gibbon's history, says Michener) bring us out of total immersion in the past to present values and judgments.

A more important structural consideration is the relationship of parts among the twelve chapters that make up the historical panorama. Michener tells us that the twelve chapters issued fully formed from the brow of Jove one April morning in 1970, and Kings reports that "He felt that all the chapters were essential stones in the total arch of *Centennial*," even though "they covered radically different ground."[3] In fact, they are unequal in dramatic unity as well as in usefulness to the basic themes. Most readers feel that the novel goes on too long, that Chapters 12 and 13 are a kind of addendum containing material it would be better to let Vernor handle briefly in Chapter 14.

The setting for the narratives is principally the region of the South Platte River in northeastern Colorado, chosen partly because Michener knew it well, but mostly because it is average, unglamorous, and therefore representative of western settlement. Each chapter has a map (or chart) at the beginning. There is recurring mention of the chief features of the landscape: Chalk Cliffs, where the skeleton of diplodocus (a dinosaur) was discovered in 1875; Beaver Mountain; Blue Valley, where there is gold; Rattlesnake Buttes, eroded fingers of a one-time mesa; and always the South Platte, the dullest river in America.

In the second and third chapters we are given the geological history of the region and an account of the appearance of the primitive creatures that inhabited it for millions of years. As in *Hawaii*, Michener is a master of lucid and often dramatic exposition of how this land was made and populated. The general outlines of the process are verifiable. The time span involved is subject to wild speculative variation. Constant alterations of the earth's surface took place during two billion years of only inferential record.

When man did finally arrive on the scene, he would be the inheritor of those vanished years, and everything he did would be limited to some degree by what had happened to his earth in those forgotten years, for it was then that its quality was determined, its mineral content, the value of its soil and salinity of its waters.

What is impressed upon us throughout this prehistory is the dog-eat-dog battle for survival among the many species. We meet the great dinosaur who died at Chalk Cliffs some 136,000,000 years ago. Paleohippus, the postulated progenitor of eohippus, came into being in that region and emigrated to Asia by way of the Bering bridge. About 800,000 years later the first bison came *from* Asia. The first to come died, but about 6,000 B.C. a new breed came to throng the plains. Rufous (with whom Michener says he identifies) is the protagonist here in epic fights and epic rutting. On one occasion, part of the herd in a tremendous stampede tumbles over the Chalk Cliffs. Twelve thousand bison die, sharing an epic burial ground with diplodocus. Beaver develop in the region, and we are made privy to a cave they built, which we will see again as the tomb of a murdered man in the nineteenth century. Eagles and prairie dogs and rattlers come into being and do battle at Rattlesnake Buttes.

Finally man comes to the area: "It was a cruel land, that year when men arrived," Michener writes. But it was beautiful. "The vast plains had a nobility that would never diminish, for they were a challenge." The mountains' majesty was also a challenge. "Centennial, when it was founded, would look eastward and catch the full power of the prairie, or westward to the Rockies." Its inhabitants would be faced with the impossible task of reconciling the demands of mountains and plains:

Many would destroy themselves in this conflict, but those who survived, assimilating the best of these two contrasting worlds, would attain a largeness of soul that other men who chose easier paths would not discover.

This introduction to the epic of *Centennial* makes promises that it does not fail to keep. It also contains a warning of the dangers and disappointment that attend the struggle. In days gone by our ancestors performed doughty deeds of daring and endurance, but also of cunning, cruelty, and deceit.

It is not clear *when* human beings came to the west of North America. Certainly there was an incursion by boat around 6000 B.C., but some three thousand years before that a huntsman skilled in the making of flint heads killed a mammoth entombed at Chalk Cliffs. His spear was still in the mammoth when its carcass was dug up in the nineteenth century. We do know that as the white man pushed in from the east in the eighteenth and nineteenth centuries, Indians from that area were pushed on into the plains. From Minnesota one group wandered to the Platte River region. It is they who become the prime example of Indian life and culture for this novel; they are known as the Arapaho, or as "Our People," in their tongue.

To begin with, they have neither horses nor guns. In 1768 the legendary Lame Beaver steals twenty-nine horses from the Comanche along the Arkansas River to the south. By this feat the horse is brought back to Rattlesnake Buttes, where he had originated millions of years before. In 1782 Lame Beaver wrests a gun from a Pawnee, but he has no ammunition and makes the mistake of breaking it by clubbing a snake. Later on the Arapaho go up into the mountains to Blue Valley, where in an encounter with the Utes they acquire a gun and gold-nugget bullets as well as tent poles. In 1803 Lame Beaver stakes himself out (a pledge not to run away) in a foray against the Pawnee. He dies "at the end of an epoch, the grandest the western Indians were to know." In their new home the Arapaho tribe had found the horse and the gun and had developed a wild, sweeping pattern of life. The narrator wonders, with excessive enthusiasm, if there had ever been in America "another group of a thousand men who left so deep an imprint upon the image of the Nation?"

To some readers at least, interesting though this account of Indian life is, the story does not really come alive until two white men come on scene in 1799. They are officially introduced in Chapter 5, "The Yellow Apron." Pasquinel is a *coureur de bois*; that is, a loner who is happiest in the wilds. Alexander McKeag has fled from Scotland after an accidental murder. He is nineteen. Pasquinel is twenty-six. Their activities span almost the first half of the nineteenth century, filling the period from Indian domination to their subjection by the encroaching white men. The epic prowess of those two men is even more prodigious than that of Lame Beaver, though in the long perspective of time their feats too are writ on sand. They are such imposing figures that we would like to know more about them, but we are allowed only to observe them. Pasquinel seeks no emotional rewards in life but receives the devotion of at least two wives, one in St. Louis and the other, Clay Basket, on the frontier. McKeag, a more complex being, comes to learn the anguish of loneliness and in his turn he is rewarded by the love of Clay Basket, who years earlier had tended him after a nearly fatal wound and had convinced him he must shoot a gun in spite of the pain from the wound, since that was the only way he could survive in the wilderness.

Pasquinel's formula for getting along with the Indians is "Never fight the Indian if you can avoid it. Never betray him in a trade. Bring him to you by faithfulness." On the whole, this formula works, until, after many years, he is killed by the encroaching Shoshoni. McKeag's formula, or uncontemplated response, is to learn the many Indian languages he encounters and to speak to the Indians in their own tongues. There is a tenuous stability in this relationship, imperiled early by the conflicting loyalties of the two sons of Pasquinel and Clay Basket, Jacques and Marcel, known as Jake and Mike. A tremendous fight takes place between Jake and McKeag at the 1827 rendezvous of the mountain men in Idaho. There we witness the brawling bonhomie of the lonely explorers and exploiters and witness the beginnings of a racial conflict that can only end in violence.

At this point the center of the narrative is the open collision between vanishing Indian and increasingly dominant settler, the subject of Chapters 6 and 7. The chief characters here are among the most memorable in the novel, although again we see them mostly from the outside. We are in the year 1844 in the Pennsylvania Dutch country around Lancaster, Pennsylvania. Speech and mores of this region bear the stamp of close and loving observation by Michener, who indicates a deep sympathy for the resentment of young Levi Zendt against the tyrannical bigotry of his brothers and his commu-

nity. At the age of twenty-four he is condemned and
ostracized for a harmless attempt at flirtation. The Reverend Fenstermacher (who opens *no* windows to freedom), a guest at the Zendts' Sunday dinner, declares
that "A man like this should go and live amongst the
savages." Levi does, taking with him sixteen-year-old
Elly from the local orphanage, who is as resentful as he
over the narrow outlook of the community. (One of the
other girls at the orphanage says that Elly is escaping
for all of them.) The young couple take vows before a
minister—not quite a formal marriage, since they do
not take time to go to the county seat for a license, but
enough to legalize connubial love.

The two Zendts then embark with their team and
Conestoga wagon at Pittsburgh on April 1, 1844, making their way to St. Louis and then up the Missouri by
riverboat. They meet a Captain Maxwell Mercy, who
is on his way to establish an army fort in the Platte
region. (He, it happens, is married to Lisette Pasquinel,
daughter to Pasquinel's St. Louis wife.) With the party
are some Vermont religious fanatics who are thoroughly
disagreeable and who slow down progress by refusing
to travel on Sunday. At Independence the travelers are
joined by Oliver Seccombe, a young Englishman of
twenty-six who has illusions about Indians being noble
savages, and by Sam Purchas, a disreputable mountain
man who will guide them to Oregon. Purchas feeds the
travelers tales about Indian depredations (including those
of the Pasquinel brothers) and kills Indians on sight. He
also attempts to rape Elly, and when he leaves the travelers steals nearly all they have.

Arrival at the confluence of the Laramie and the
Platte occurs at a time when

the two races approached a state of equilibrium: the Indians
still owned the land and still controlled it, the buffalo were
plentiful, and white soldiers had not yet begun to shoot at
Indians they were fearful of, and peace was still possible.

From that point on, the Indians, as their situation declines, will suffer not only hostility but degradation. The lines of the conflict become clearly drawn among the fictional characters. In a parley over where to build the fort, Captain Mercy is remarkably diplomatic in contrast to Purchas, who tries to shoot Jake in the back. (Jake is Mercy's brother-in-law.)

The Zendts turn back after crossing the Continental Divide, because of Levi's premonitions of disaster and because Elly is pregnant. They join forces with Alexander McKeag and set up a store at what becomes the town of Zendt's Farm at the confluence of Beaver Creek and the South Platte. (This town in turn will rename itself Centennial.) After Elly dies from a rattlesnake bite, Levi takes up with Lucinda, the daughter of Clay Basket and Pasquinel. But she is uncertain of her place in the world, tries out the social whirl of St. Louis, where she is kindly received by Pasquinel's other family and is the belle of the ball for a season. Soon she elects to come back to the prairie and marry Levi, finding her true identity in the mixed life of the frontier.

Chapter 7, "The Massacre," is a meticulous account of cruelty on the part of individuals and of bad faith on the part of government. Up to 1851 less than one-tenth of one percent of the immigrants had been killed by Indians. "For this good record the Indian was mostly responsible, for it was his willingness to abide the white man that allowed the two groups to coexist in such harmony." In 1851 a great meeting is convened to forge treaties with the various Indian tribes, whom the Supreme Court had ruled to be nations. Major Mercy, as chief negotiator, encounters various points of view among the Indians, in addition to the traditional inter-tribal enmities that make them distrust each other. In spite of an administrative foul-up, by which $50,000 worth of government gifts and food is delayed and about 14,000 Indians and some 30,000 horses are left on the verge of starvation, there is amicable discussion, and a relatively fair set of treaties is drawn up. Mercy, however, is deficient in not realizing that the empty plains will soon attract farmers and that therefore the Indian settlements of land will not hold. The treaties may have been made by men of integrity but they are carried out by "meanspirited" government functionaries. Indeed, the U.S. Senate never ratifies the whole of the 1851 treaty and "the Indians [are] left with no secure title to their land."

Events take a rapid and disastrous course. A drifter named Larkin finds gold in Blue Valley. Within weeks it is lined solid with claims. Ultimately $19,000,000 worth of gold is taken out; than it becomes a ghost town, one of the ugliest on earth. Furthermore, the pouring in of prospectors has undermined the treaty by dooming the buffalo and encouraging usurpation of Indian lands. Such pressures bring about a new and bad treaty, reducing the nomadic Indians to forty-acre allotments. On November 4, 1863—with heavy irony, just two weeks before the Gettysburg Address—Mercy writes that 1863 is a year of starvation for the Indians. In 1864 there is a series of killings and retaliations. Forty-three Indians are killed for one missing white-owned horse.

What follows might be called the fascist reign of Frank Skimmerhorn, members of whose family in Minnesota had been killed by Indians. A self-designated colonel, he heads up a vigilante movement in Colorado, for to him extermination of Indians is "both a duty and an exaltation." Though not a Mormon, he is much taken with the Mormon identification of the Indians with the Lost Tribes and thus feels his war is sanctified. He conscripts local militia with himself in command. He moves his forces to Rattlesnake Buttes, arrests the Zendts for consorting with the enemy, and massacres a group of Arapaho who are peaceably encamped where the government is supposed to protect and feed them. One of his officers, Captain Reed, refuses to attack. This brings an investigation by General Wade, in the course of which a soldier gives testimony so shocking that Skimmerhorn is rebuked and Reed exonerated. For his honesty the soldier is ambushed and shot.

Jake Pasquinel's response is to promise war and burning and murder all along the Platte. Skimmerhorn, still inflamed with fanaticism, sets fire to the prairie, consuming nearly all the edible fodder from the Platte to the Arkansas. Jake is captured, given a drumhead trial, and hanged. Levi, having gone to retrieve his brother-in-law's body, has his store burned; then he and Lucinda try to save Jake's brother Mike by having him give himself up. On the way to the sheriff Mike is shot in the back by Skimmerhorn. After an errand of mercy Major Mercy receives a terrible beating. In an editorial comment at the end of the chapter historian Vernor singles out Peter Held, editor of the local paper, as a man convinced of manifest destiny who preached that the sooner "the irresistible forces of nationalism" prevailed, the better. In his paper Held thus incited the vigilante action against the Indians and later against the sheepmen, as his counterparts in the twentieth century would do against striking coal miners or those who sought to defend the natural resources of the state.

The most unified and therefore the most memorable section of the novel is Chapter 8, "The Cowboys," which leads into the third broad phase of this work: settlement of the West. As the conflict with the Indians recedes, a vast new enterprise begins, the bringing of cattle to the prairie range. In 1867, Oliver Seccombe, coming from Oregon twenty-three years after we first met him, begins to build up the great Venneford Ranch with capital from a group of British investors in Bristol.[4] By terms of the Homestead Act of 1862, land not taken up by settlers remained free for casual use. Thus, by acquiring seventeen crucial water sites, Seccombe rapidly creates a vast holding in which ownership of less than 3,000 acres permits control of 5,670,000 acres of range (an area larger than Massachusetts). The next step is to stock the range with cattle. John Skimmerhorn, a fine young man of twenty-nine burdened with his repudiated father's hated name, undertakes to go to Texas to acquire longhorns and bring them back. In Texas he engages R. J. Poteet, a Civil War veteran, to be the mastermind of the enterprise.

There follows a detailed and authentic picture of cowboy activity and manners, better than anything else of its kind in fiction because it is accurate and down-to-earth. The crew is a varied one: Ignacio Gómez, an unemployed cook who has to prove himself in order to overcome Poteet's prejudice against Mexicans; Nate Person, an ex-slave; Mule Canby, who sells them his horses for $85 and is one of the most skilled in directing the drive; Buford Coker, another down-on-his-luck veteran, from South Carolina, who talks himself into a job though he has never ridden. As they set forth, they add Jim Lloyd, a boy of fourteen, whose father is dead and whose mother realizes that he must go out into the world of men. He becomes a principal character in the central portion of the novel, and one of the most engaging.

In order to avoid marauding Apaches along the way, Poteet undertakes a detour to the south and west through a desert, the *llano estacado* (that is, "the plain set with stakes" to guide the way), and then north through New Mexico, over the Raton Pass, and into Colorado. The desert crossing is an ordeal, but they survive with little loss. In an encounter at a crossing of the Pecos River, Jim Lloyd kills an Indian. Canby loses an arm and has to be left behind at an army post. When a greedy mountain man tries to levy an extortionate toll at Raton Pass, Poteet finds another route. Crossing the Arkansas River is their most difficult undertaking, but they lose only eleven cattle. In a fight with the Pettis gang of outlaws Coker rescues Jim. They meet a gigantic herd of buffalo, one of the last, and manage to keep the cattle from stampeding—only to lose a good many two nights later when there is a stampede. As they near their destination, they come upon the starving Arapaho, to whom they give three steers. Lost Eagle is both pathetic and dignified in his last days.

Jim Lloyd is sad as the journey ends and the crew breaks up. Such a group, he believes, if held together, could forge a good life for themselves. But though lack of social cohesion is a major weakness of the West, feats of valor can be carried out in concert, as this episode shows. Certainly it exhibits and celebrates leadership, skill, responsibility, courage, and ingenuity. These are characteristics that make possible the winning of the West, even though it is being won—temporarily at least—for absentee owners and foreign capitalists.

Another major and representative figure in the settlement of Colorado is Hans "Potato" Brumbaugh, who appears in Chapter 9. He comes from a German settlement in the Ukraine by way of Illinois, seeking gold but ending by finding wealth in farming. Brumbaugh buys land from Levi Zendt and incurs the opposition of Seccombe, who is accustomed to running interlopers off. One night Levi and Brumbaugh kill one of the hired thugs who are threatening Potato and run off the others. Levi comments wisely that in a fight for the land the farmer will always kill off the rancher, because the farmer is tied to the land and will fight to protect it. Not only does Brumbaugh fight for his land, he tends it with unequaled passion. Whereas a small group of neighboring Wyoming cattlemen in the Cheyenne Club dominate the Wyoming legislature and are ruthless in protecting their interests, Brumbaugh and others have a much broader vision. They, in their turn, tap British capital to build canals to irrigate the starving land.

Brumbaugh even dreams of tunneling through the mountains to bring water from west of the divide, a dream that will be fulfilled in the next century. He also has the idea of growing sugar beets. This brings into being a new and temporarily dominant agricultural activity, for beets also feed cattle as the range runs out.

Still a third claimant to the bounty of the land comes in the person of Messmore Garrett, who has the effrontery to bring in sheep. The cowboys are revolted, and a war develops. By glacierlike pressure the sheepmen acquire some parcels of land. Levi Zendt sells them two thousand acres at Chalk Cliffs. In retaliation his store is set afire. The expanding sheepmen set up squatters on the eastern rim of the Venneford Ranch and homesteaders along the Platte. The Pettis gang become paid killers, stampeding sheep and killing Buford Coker and his common-law wife. Jim Lloyd and Brumbaugh take the law into their own hands and kill the Pettis boys in full daylight. Somehow no witnesses of the killing are to be found.

One strand of narrative not strictly relevant to the broad development of the novel is that which concerns Charlotte Buckland, the daughter of one of the shareholders in Venneford Ranch. Her father brings her to America on a business trip, and she is fascinated by the new country. Having turned down the proposal of a St. Louis Pasquinel, she becomes interested in Oliver Seccombe and ultimately marries him. They occupy the magnificent if inappropriate castle he has built on the ranch with funds more or less misappropriated from the business. When some years later Seccombe avoids disgrace by committing suicide, she marries Jim Lloyd and with him manages the ranch for nearly twenty years.

With Chapter 11, "The Crime," we have come to the culmination of the epic narrative, for this tangential episode provides by its dramatic unity a useful commentary as it shows the criminal roots of respectability in a lawless age. This is stated bluntly by the narrative voice:

There was a dark side to western history, and many a family that later attained prominence did so only because some enterprising progenitor had known when to strike and how to keep his mouth shut.

The account of a murder and cover-up by the Marvin Wendells and their ten-year-old son Philip, and the effort of the sheriff to solve the crime, is good melodrama, especially when the remnants of the Pettis gang come to town and shoot the sheriff down before he can work on the boy to tell the truth. The relevance of this chapter is strengthened by the fact that in the book's final chapter Philip's son, who is running for office, is concerned that bringing up this ancient crime might ruin his chances.

As indicated earlier, the last two chapters of the historical narrative are a letdown. Michener attempts to do too much in too little space, and he has to introduce a complete new set of characters to conduct even a truncated action.

One subject of this twentieth-century phase is the problem of getting workers for the fields: no sooner do they arrive than they are bitten by the desire to *own* land, exactly in the way that Potato Brumbaugh yearned for ownership. Brumbaugh tries Japanese workers, who outdo him in capacity for work and in land-owning zeal. Jim Lloyd remembers the Mexican cook on the cattle drive long ago and undertakes to bring field workers from Mexico. This is certainly an important part of the history of Colorado, but too much attention is paid to the Mexican revolutions of the early part of the century and to the involvement of Tranquilino Marquez in that violence.

The climactic event in the saga of the land—and its proper ending—is the arrival of an agronomist who is an advocate of dry farming. His ideas are eagerly espoused by the railroad and by Marvin Wendell, now a persuasive real estate promoter. The novel contends that the land-use system of 1911 was "one of the most advantageous in the world," establishing "a neat balance between the needs of man and the dictates of nature." But advocacy of dry farming brought in a wave of new immigrants imbued with the "authentic vision of the pioneer American, the dream of freedom and more spacious horizons." Jim Lloyd and Potato Brumbaugh, patriarchs of the old order, are also prophets of doom of the new. They warn the newcomers that the first crop, the sod crop, is a sure thing, but that after that when the rainfall is below normal, when the winds begin to blow, disaster will strike. In the 1920s luck deserts the area. Only a few learn the lesson of contour plowing, so that when in 1931 ominous winds like tornadoes hit the plains, the soil turns to dust. In time both cattle raising and the sugar beet industry will have to give up and the land revert to its original state.

In Chapter 14, "November Elegy," we come back to the contemporary frame narrative, where much of the content of the two preceding chapters could and should have been more economically accommodated. Vernor becomes closely associated with Paul Garrett, age forty-six, a leader in many fields, whom the governor has named to head the Colorado centennial celebration. Much too neatly, the Garrett genealogical chart shows Paul to be descended from the Messmore Garretts, Levi and Lucinda Pasquinel Zendt, Red Wolf and Pale Star, Maxwell and Lisette Pasquinel Mercy, John Skimmerhorn, and Jim and Charlotte Buckland Lloyd. He has the grace to fall in love with and marry Flor Marquez, the great-granddaughter of Tranquilino Marquez. Garrett takes Vernor with him as he travels over the state in preparation for the centennial celebrations. He discourses on the need to control natural resources

intelligently, being willing to allow ski resorts if enough
primitive area is "held inviolable." He calls the man who
is found not guilty of shooting bald eagles and killing
bears "a one-man ecological disaster." He shows Vernor
the South Platte from the air, a pure stream near its
source, a sewer in Denver.

Reflecting on the conditions of life undergone by
the first wave of settlers, Garrett thinks that loneliness
is the national malady. Though it encouraged ingenuity
and drive, it has had a heavy social cost. After their
marriage he and Flor visit "the family"—that is, the
remaining Arapaho—who now live in Wyoming. Reflecting that there is nothing to be done for the Indians,
Garrett asserts, "The way we react to the Indian will
always remain the nation's unique moral headache."
Other nations have solved like problems, often brutally.
"Only in America did we show total confusion." He is
willing to concede that it was inevitable that the land
should be taken from the Indian. "The white man was
in motion, the Indian wasn't." He believes that reser-
vation land should now be distributed among the Indians, who would then have to sink or swim in the
dominant culture.

The most luminous figure in this final chapter is
Cisco, "the last of the real cowboys, the last of the
buffalo men." As he sings his famous songs, he becomes
something larger than life, "an epic figure chanting in
the darkness of the wide, free days that were no more."
But this is retrospective. As the novel ends Paul Garrett
is drunk at the Railway Arms in Centennial, having felt
sick to his stomach that afternoon, as he watched the
Simmenthals, a new breed of cattle, move out to take
possession of land which for a century had reverberated
to the hoofbeats of Herefords. He becomes increasingly
mournful over the future of Centennial: "It [has] known
a good hundred years and now [is] perishing." No one

around seems to remember the past or to be interested in it. Later that evening Cisco comes and grieves along with him, insisting that for better or worse, their roots are there, that "a man springs from the soil but he don't spring far." And: "I live in Centennial because it's maybe the best spot in America...could even be the best remainin' spot on earth." Garrett echoes him: "Could be. It damn well could be."

Until recently Michener stories did not fare well at the hands of moviemakers, and with the advent of his block-busters it looked as though nothing significent on film could be done. In the late 1970s producer John Wilder took up the challenge embodied in *Centennial* and trans-lated that work to film to produce a masterpiece.

For once Hollywood superlatives were justified. The film was faithful to the novel and at the same time tran-scended it by using the additional dimensions of cine-matic technique. The scenic background was authentic and brilliantly reproduced. The casting was superb, the acting perfect. To mention only three unforgettable per-formances, Robert Gordon as Pasquinel, Richard Chamberlain as McKeag, and Barbara Carrera as Clay Basket fixed those personalities forever in the mind of the American audience. The movie is probably more epic than the novel in its sweeping panorama of the developing West. It justified every minute of the twenty-five hours' showing time it called for, not to mention the upward of $25,000,000 it took to make the film.[5] We can only hope that in time *Chesapeake* will be the beneficiary of equally dedicated treatment. Then Mich-ener will add to his laurels the existence of two mas-terpieces on film.

Chesapeake

Not quite on home ground, but close enough, Michener infuses this 1978 novel with a sense of the wonder of nature and a nostalgia for the simplicity of the past. *Chesapeake*, to be sure, says much more than that. It is certainly a superior novelistic summing up of the making of America on the Eastern Seaboard. It is also a celebration of courage, physical courage on the part of the early settlers and the later "watermen," moral courage on the part of the Quaker settlers and their descendants. Nearly four hundred years of history are surveyed, from the solitary incursion of a peaceful Indian of the Susquehannock tribe in 1583 to the 1978 funeral of a Quaker who killed himself in shame after involvement in the Watergate scandal. It has an almost Götterdämmerung finale, as on their return from the funeral blacks and whites and watermen press together in unaccustomed solidarity while a hurricane roars about them and the last vestige of Devon Island disappears beneath the waves.

As is his custom, Michener has chosen an unstoried, run-of-the-mill locale in which to place his narrative. The Choptank River on the Eastern Shore of Chesapeake Bay exists. Devon Island and the town of Patamoke are fictional, though Cambridge, Maryland, across from Patamoke is real (and was much in the news during the desegregation disturbances of the 1960s). The region, until very recently, was an almost exclusively maritime world, an insular world, accessible only by boat, cut off from the main action of political and social life in Virginia, in Baltimore and Annapolis, and in Washington on the western side of the bay. It was not until 1952 that a bridge from Annapolis to the Eastern Shore was built. It was not until 1964 that north–south travel could cross the mouth of the great bay by bridge to tidewater Virginia. In recent decades people of wealth from the centers of power have created estates on the Eastern Shore, but even so, there is a residual simplicity in this out-of-the-way region, and something timeless about it. It is not an Eden, for violence and folly have always flourished there, but in its anachronistic simplicity it reminds us of a more primitive way of life.

In this work, as in its predecessors, historical personages have very little place. John Smith as the first begetter of America is on stage at the beginning. We even get a thumbnail sketch of this able and impossible little man. There are contacts with Tom Jefferson and George Washington and with a dandified General Lafayette. Henry Clay, Daniel Webster, and John Calhoun all come to Devon Island to stay with the Steeds and set forth their political philosophies or forward their interests. The novel could probably do without these historical builders of the nation, but they do buttress the authenticity of the narrative by their presence.

The organization of episodes departs somewhat from that used in Michener's previous novels. For one thing, he is at long last content with a straightforward third-person omniscient narrator. We do not, therefore, have to adjust to a shifting point of view, though there are occasions when narrative flow is impeded by fairly heavy doses of narrator information. Occasions also arise when there is resort to straightforward dramatic dialogue as in a play. These passages are not sustained for long, but they seem unnecessarily artificial.

The suspension of a first-person approach permits a kind of double-headed arrangement for each of the fourteen episodes. First we have a numbered "Voyage" section. This is a brief narrative (only two of them are over twenty pages in length) in which a character or situation is introduced at a specific time and place. Each "Voyage," except the last one, is followed by a titled narrative of considerable length, less unified and generally less dramatic than the introductory "Voyage."

The "Voyages" also serve as a continuous reminder of the maritime nature of this world, reinforced, in typical Michener fashion, by introductory maps.

If we ignore for the moment this fourteen-fold division, we can see that the novel falls into three unequal parts. The first seven episodes are loosely concerned with the settlement of the Eastern Shore by Britain and then its ultimate severing from that nation. This culminates in a duel of two ships at sea in which the British vessel is lured to self-destruction. The next three episodes focus brilliantly on the heightening conflict over slavery before the outbreak of the Civil War, although that problem has been a preoccupation of the Paxmore family from the beginning. As usual, Michener finds it hard to give unity to the end of his novel. The last episodes are diverse in tone and subject as they attempt to show the impact of larger experience on the region. They do at least succeed in suggesting a degree of timelessness in the midst of change.

The fictional dramatis personae are four major families, three of which come to the Eastern Shore in the first decades of the seventeenth century. The fourth is an ex-slave family which has ironically been given the name of Cater, a character who was a fierce advocate of slavery and who moved to the Carolinas. These families provide a nice mixture of the heroic search for order and the recalcitrant defiance of order. The first of these newcomers is a Catholic, Edmund Steed, who, to get away from the falseness of his position in England, joins John Smith on his 1607 voyage. From the James River settlement Steed also goes along on a voyage to explore Chesapeake Bay in search of the elusive route to the Indies. He is entranced by Choptank River and Devon Island. Knowing that he will always be uncomfortable pretending in Virginia to be a member of the Church of England, he is determined to strike out on his own at the first opportunity.

Michener gives a fine account of the testing time of the James River colony from Captain Smith's departure until the arrival of rescue ships in May 1610. A year later Steed makes his great gamble, going alone to the Choptank and establishing himself on "the island of Devon, proprietary to the Steeds." In September a band of Indians, headed by Pentaquod, a refugee Susquehannock, make contact with him. A deed is signed, not only for the two thousand acres of the island but for another two thousand acres of shore land. The Indians cannot understand why Steed refuses the offer of Pentaquod's daughter as his wife. On one of his trips to Virginia he encounters the disillusioned imported bride of Simon Janney, an unedifying planter on the Rappahannock. She accompanies Steed to Devon, lives with "the bloody Papist," and produces a son, Ralph, in 1616. She leaves without rancor when Martha Keene, a Catholic girl of twenty-two, arrives from England to be Edmund's wife. Since there is no priest available, they make do with a wedding arranged by Pentaquod, while his daughter looks on disconsolate. Ultimately, when Maryland becomes a separate colony under the proprietorship of the Catholic Calvert family, the couple are married by a priest and their children baptized.

Settlers in this new colony are determined not to allow a theocracy, such as existed in New England. They want no sectarian disputes. Indeed, Catholics are urged not to be aggressive or ostentatious about their faith. However, laws are enacted against Jews and others who deny the Trinity. At a meeting called by Lord Baltimore, Steed takes the lead in insisting that laws be enacted by democratic process, not by proprietary fiat. As he returns from the Western Shore victorious, he dies of a heart attack. The last thing he sees is the erosion that has already begun to undermine Devon Island.

The second family line is that of the Turlocks. Nothing could be more different from the Steed line than they. Timothy Turlock, a London thief, has been compassionately saved from hanging and sent instead to Virginia as an indentured servant. Unfortunately, he has received Simon Janney as his master. Once he has been to the Eastern Shore, he is determined to return there, and he runs off with his master's shallop and goes to live with the Indians. All this occurs a generation after Steed's arrival. Turlock develops a passionate love of the land and the rivers, intuitively sensing what he must do to live with them. When a severe winter forces him to seek out the Steeds, he is granted sanctuary in spite of his bad reputation. He buys a tract from the Indians, later altering the map so that he may claim an additional two hundred acres. He registers the deed with the Steeds and steals equipment from them at every opportunity. A complete scoundrel, he thinks only of his own advantage, marrying Pentaquod's daughter but sending her away when he finds a lusty Swedish girl who has run away from a brutal master. In all, this unappetizing scoundrel sires six bastards, the beginning of the horde of Turlocks who would love and prosper in this watery world. Through six generations none of them would learn to read or write, and they would be an affront, as well as an attraction, to the Steeds, and a challenge to the Quaker Paxmores, the third major family line.

Edward Paxmore, a religious nonconformist, has been in constant trouble in Massachusetts Bay Colony. In 1661 he is swayed toward Quakerism by the example of Thomas Kenworthy, who is lashed and ultimately hanged as part of the official effort to root out the "pernicious heresy" of Quakerism. After his conversion Paxmore is whipped out of town after town and into Rhode Island, which is more tolerant of heresy, only to return again to Massachusetts to face down authority. He joins Ruth Brinton, another Quaker, whose courage and suffering are even greater than his. He believes she has died

from her whippings. Finally Judge Goddard is so worn
down by Paxmore's reappearances that he urges him to
go to the new colony of Maryland, which he can reach
only by way of Barbados.

On that island Paxmore learns about the traffic in
slaves but takes little interest in it, for to him slavery is
merely lifelong indenture and not necessarily more cruel
or unreasonable than what happens to white men. When
he finally reaches the Choptank, he is greeted by Henry
Steed and goes on to join the small cluster of Quakers
at Patamoke. There he finds Ruth Brinton, who is nearly
dead from the whippings she has received but who recovers because of his presence. They marry and go to
live on the cliff on which Pentaquod had landed eighty-
one years before. They call their dwelling Peace Cliff,
and it is a beacon of belief in freedom that will shine
out for the next two centuries. Paxmore, a skilled car-
penter, builds a meetinghouse for his brethren and helps
the Steeds with his skills, but he is soon drawn by an
unexpected ambition: he wants to build ships. Clumsy
at first, he learns by doing. His sober, industrious life
is based on a simple creed: "After obedience to God,
faithful performance of one's job is what counts."

Ironically, the first slaves on the Eastern Shore are
Paxmore's, a consignment sent in payment for work
done in Barbados. Ruth is against slavery from the start.
The argument that to free slaves is to undermine property rights has no validity to her mind. She charges the
Patamoke Quakers to end slavery and is rebuffed by the
Meeting, who hear her tolerantly and turn her down
unanimously. She transfers the slaves to the Steeds in
the expectation that they will have more opportunities
on that large and varied plantation. Her good intentions
are thwarted when the slaves are sold away from Devon.
She receives a signal lesson about the "disaster which
the good people of this river would always bring down

on themselves." She does not give up her crusade to end slavery, a crusade that is carried on, especially by Paxmore women, for two hundred years.

"Voyage Five: 1701" shows the relationship of the three contrasted families after a couple of generations. Rosalind Janney, the less-than-glamorous great-granddaughter of Simon Janney on the Rappahannock, makes an arranged marriage with Fitzhugh Steed. She is twenty-six; he is forty. He has two children by a previous marriage, and the new marriage produces three more. Fitzhugh has a Turlock inamorata and spends a minimum of time with his wife. Rosalind, who admires Ruth Brinton Paxmore, determines to be strong. She tells Fitzhugh that he is no longer her husband but must continue to be her protector. She will take over the management of the estate, for she is determined that all the Steeds shall work and learn. When the Fithian firm in London wants her to intervene and save the improvident Janneys from bankruptcy because of their feckless incompetence, she is outraged at the wastage of husbands and wives by pampered, indolent plantation life.

Her stepson, Mark Steed, whom she thinks of as "the salvation of the Steeds," comes home from his European education in a convoy of two hundred sailing vessels, so great is the danger from pirates. He marries Amanda Paxmore. Rosalind's two little boys are taken to a Jesuit monastery at the head of Chesapeake Bay to begin their education. When she and Mark return from that voyage, they are set upon by pirates. Mark and her daughter are killed; the plantation buildings are burned. The pirate Bonfleur, who had posed as a Quaker while visiting the colony some months before, gloats over his success. Rosalind and others vow vengeance. When Bonfleur is caught, he is, at her insistence, brought to Patamoke for hanging.

Rosalind becomes a power in the community and something of a feminist, inveighing against the public whipping of women as an act of lust. She defies the authorities and is joined by Ruth Paxmore and Nelly Turlock in baring their bodies to the public gaze when the sentence on another woman is carried out. This leads to conflict with the magistrate, Broadnax, and Rosalind herself is brought to trial for, as she sees it, "offenses against the male community." Convicted, she is subjected to a perfunctory ducking and given an ovation by her friends. During this period she has been gradually erecting a brick house consisting of three separate cubes, ultimately joined by two glassed-in breezeways. Until it is finished, the building is considered a monstrosity and receives the name "Rosalind's Revenge." Completed, however, its harmonious balance is evident and it becomes, in spite of its name, the epitome of gracious living in the South. It is fitting that after such a stormy life Rosalind should die in a storm as she stubbornly makes a short journey on the Choptank River.

The most engrossing section of the novel is "Voyage Six: 1773," followed by "The Three Patriots." This narrative gives a remarkably convincing insight into the human elements in the American Revolution. In 1770 one Jonathan Wilcok is appointed rector of the Anglican Church at Wrentham, Maryland. He is a tyrant and a greedy man, "two hundred pounds of blackmail, simony, and self-indulgence." Simon Steed, age forty-three, and Levin Paxmore, age forty, as Catholic and Quaker respectively refuse to tithe. Teach Turlock, age forty-one, a waterman of no religion and a potential revolutionary, also withstands the rector. All three are brought to trial, convicted, and ordered to pay up. To do so Turlock would have to surrender some of his land. He goes to jail. Eventually he gives in to pressure and signs two copies of a deed, which are then stolen. He declares a "private war against the English" and becomes a privateer in his black sloop.

Though of widely different social origins and phi-

losophies these three representatives of the Eastern Shore
are temporarily bound together in their opposition to
English heavy-handedness. Even though conservative
landowner Steed recognizes that hotheads like Turlock
are a danger to everyone and fears that good subjects
"will be pushed to the wall by the canaille," he is willing
to admit that society depends on judicious compromise.
Steed also recognizes that, if war does come, it will be
to his advantage to have a fleet of ships, of course under
the British flag. He wants Paxmore immediately to build
him an armed schooner for the protection of his ship-
ping. Paxmore has moral reservations about building a
warship, but compromises, telling himself that he is
building it as a Quaker pacifist. Of the three only Turlock is all out for war with Britain, but events bring it
about that they become firm and even famous allies in
the conduct of the American Revolution.

A complicating factor in Steed's response is his marriage to Jane Fithian. When in 1774 her brother sends
Steed a shipload of tea on which a very low tax has been
imposed, she prevents her husband's taking advantage
of this special opportunity, because to sell at retail means
that one is in trade, which is beneath the dignity of
gentlemen. Paxmore is, on principle, against any tax.
Turlock takes the law into his own hands, capturing the
ship and in time burning it as a symbolic defiance of
England. Maryland is up in arms. Steed chairs a meeting
from which there issues a bill of complaint, softened by
assurances of allegiance to the Crown.

Turlock's ship is destroyed in a fight with the British. He is saved by an American privateer. He gets a
new ship, which the Virginia authorities take away from
him. Steed then lets him captain his own *Whisper*, even
though he is uneasy over tolerating what used to be
called piracy and is now looked upon as patriotism.
Turlock captures four ships in 1776, but four Paxmore-
built vessels are lost. To Ellen Paxmore this is proof

that her husband should not build ships of war. Jane Fithian Steed, increasingly anticolonial, demands to go back to England with her child Penny. She is repatriated on *Whisper*, with young Matt Turlock taking care of the child. Also repatriated is the rapacious rector of Wrentham, whom Turlock does not allow on board until the rector has handed over a deed to the property once ceded to him.

Steed's role in the War of Independence is an ambiguous one. He buys up depreciated currency of the Continental Congress at eighty to one, convinced that it will eventually be redeemed—as it is, to his handsome profit. His ships run the British blockade to bring needed supplies to the American forces. At this too he makes a handsome, perhaps excessive, profit. Because of his education in France he is sent to enlist the sympathies of French businessmen, traveling, of course, on *Whisper*. Turlock outwits the tight British blockade at the mouth of the Chesapeake. Teamed with Ben Franklin, Steed has some success in bringing the French business community to see the light. On his way home he goes to the Dutch West Indies to pick up cargo that has to be unloaded at Lewes, Delaware, and carried overland to the American army.

Late in 1777 the British take over the entire Chesapeake Bay area and march on Philadelphia from Havre de Grace at the head of the bay. They bombard Patamoke. Everyone, even Ellen Paxmore, works to release a nearly completed ship. In 1781 nineteen great British ships of the line are off Cape Henry on September 4. The French "by an act of supreme courage" escape the British trap. In this most critical battle of the war no Americans are engaged.

The three Patamoke families have acquitted themselves well. Steed finally serves as interpreter with the French forces at Yorktown. The Turlocks have been deadly sharpshooters, the Paxmores builders of fast ships.

At war's end unpleasant rumors spread about the war profits made by the Steeds, perhaps as much as £400,000. Thus in April 1789, when the three patriots are summoned to meet George Washington as he passes through Maryland on his way to be inaugurated in New York, the general is willing to validate Turlock's deeds, promises Paxmore that he will be paid for expenses and losses incurred, but makes it clear that Steed's reputation renders a government appointment out of the question. This whole section puts the Revolution on a matter-of-fact, nonheroic basis in a region that is largely ignored in revolutionary fiction in favor of more storied sites such as Lexington, Saratoga, Valley Forge, and the rest.

"Voyage Seven: 1811" and "The Duel" are a continuation of the maritime saga of the Revolution, with a scientific-philosophical expedition as introduction. Thomas Applegarth, an odd-job man in Patamoke, has an inquiring mind. He gets an idea of how the ice age dug out Chesapeake Bay and tries to find out more from Elizabeth Paxmore, "one of those Quaker women to whom all knowledge was important." The Paxmores add $25 to Applegarth's savings so that he can make an expedition to trace the Susquehanna to its source. When he comes at last to one of the trickly beginnings of the great river, he meditates that "This is how everything begins.... A slow accumulation—the gathering together of meaning." This statement is also a Michener accolade to simple, spontaneous American curiosity that ends in know-how.

What this expedition has to do with "The Duel" that follows is open to question. In the War of 1812 Chesapeake Bay was dominated by the British—with as many as a thousand ships at times. *Whisper*, which had been damaged, is under repair at the Paxmore yard when the British appear. Matt Turlock, whom we saw earlier as a little boy, is captain and owner of the ship. He attempts to escape out to sea, but the British find and destroy the ship, almost killing Turlock, whose arm is shot off. The enemy also find the camouflaged boatyard and burn it, bombard the town, and for good measure in passing send two cannonballs into the walls of Rosalind's Revenge. Matt Turlock commissions a new ship, *Ariel*, a clipper that is finished in 1814. He gives battle, receives heavy damage, takes refuge in St. Eustatius, a Leeward Islands port from which he engages in the illegal slave trade as a temporary measure (when the carpenters at Paxmore's yard discover that the ship is a slaver, they refuse ever to work on it again). At Belem in Brazil Turlock encounters his enemy, Captain Gatch of the British navy. He lures the British ship to chase him into a storm, where Turlock's superior seamanship and the heavy bow of the British ship cause it to go under with all hands.

"Voyage Eight: 1822" and "Widow's Walk" are the least satisfactory section of the novel and can be skipped over lightly. The daughter of the girl whom Matt Turlock took care of on a voyage to England before the Revolutionary War comes back with her mother and marries Paul Steed, a Princeton product of little drive, who shows after two centuries that the Steeds are "in danger of becoming just another tidewater family in grand decline." The wild geese which Susan observes from the high widow's walk of the Steed house sharpen her longing for a ship that will come bearing a male who will penetrate her scarcely awakened being. When the *Ariel* comes home, it is evident that Matt Turlock is avid too. The pair are equal in directness of purpose and engage in unrestrained, though outwardly decorous, fornication. Paul, the husband, takes Eden, a comely slave, to bed in retaliation. The Quakers try to bring a dash of common sense to this sexual imbroglio; Paxmore shows Susan the slave quarters on her lover's ship, but that merely excites her. Finally, Herbert, one of the mainland Steeds, takes over and confines Susan to the

island, assumes management of the plantations, and sends
Matt away. Susan resumes her watch on the widow's
walk. One day Paul knocks her over the edge and himself falls over. He soon recovers but she is an invalid.
Eden takes care of both of them. Meanwhile the erosion
of Devon Island goes on, and at the appointed season
the great geese fly home.

The most extended journey comes in "Voyage Nine:
1832." We witness the capture of slaves in the Congo
by an Arab trader. The elders of a village are not above
selling their young men, and Cudjo, a stalwart and intelligent youth of twenty-four, is so disposed of along
with twenty-six others. They walk for fifty-nine days
to the coast of Angola, where they are handed over to
the Jesuits for sale to American slavetraders. When *Ariel*,
under command of Matt Turlock, comes to pick up this
cargo, one of the Jesuits alerts the British ship that is on
patrol. Turlock eludes the ship but treats the slaves so
badly that they mount an insurrection in which he is
killed by Cudjo. Intercepted by a French ship which
turns them over to the British, the slaves and sailors are
taken to Plymouth for trial. The leaders of the insurrection are hanged, but Cudjo and some others are sent
on their way to their rightful owners in Havana, where
they are in turn sold to a brutal Georgia man who chains
them spread-eagled to the deck for their passage to the
United States.

"The Slave-Breaker," the narrative episode that follows, proceeds without interruption. General observations about slavery narrow in focus to the Eastern Shore,
which resembles a fiefdom in the Carolinas. In 1833 the
Steed holdings are over 30,000 acres; they have 683 slaves
and are proud of the way they treat them. "The pitful
fact about slavery, as it existed on the Steed plantation,"
Michener writes, "was its banality." It "pulled everyone
down to a mournful level." It degraded the whites by
making them think they were "inherently superior."

Throughout the entire social hierarchy—plantation
owners, merchants and artisans, and white trash—there
is a uniform conviction that slavery is necessary. The
Quakers are the exception. Elizabeth Paxmore actually
commits the crime of teaching black children to read.

A prime refutation of this denigration of his race,
Cudjo comes to the Steed plantation in December 1833.
He has learned in Georgia that a humble "Yassuh" is
the password to continued existence, but he is also aware
of the power of the printed word and is determined to
learn to read. He learns fast at the Paxmores' and his
zeal is his undoing. When he is caught with a book, his
Steed plantation overseer sends him to work for Herman
Cline, who has the reputation of being a slave-breaker.
In November 1836, after a grueling time, Cudjo seems
docile enough to be returned to the Steeds. He is kept
at Devon Island, where he builds a wheelchair for Susan.
Eden, who sees him as a passport to freedom, introduces
him to sex. Without Paul Steed's knowledge Eden is
sold to Cline; Paul's solution is to free her and to allow
Cudjo to work for manumission. When Herbert Steed
and Cline demand that Eden be turned over to them,
Paul fires both and resumes control of the plantations.
We conclude that the Steeds do treat their slaves better
than most.

"Voyage Ten: 1837" and "The Railroad" continue
this dramatic sketch of slavery before the Civil War.
The Paxmore son, Bartley, who had helped Cudjo learn
to read, goes up to Easton to propose to Rachel Star-
buck, whose father is an ardent abolitionist. The young
man's life is abruptly changed when he sees the help
given to runaways from Cline's farm. The following
narrative, "The Railroad," is among other things an
account of what Bartley, his wife, and others dare on
behalf of slaves, for whom crossing the Pennsylvania
border is the first step to freedom, though they are not
truly safe until they reach Canada.

In reality, in the period from 1851 to the outbreak of the war some two thousand slaves made their way up the Eastern Shore to Pennsylvania. The Dred Scott decision of the Supreme Court in the spring of 1857 destroyed the shaky compromise worked out by Senators Webster and Clay before their deaths, to the joy of "the bullheaded abolitionists who would accept nothing less than the shattering of the Union" and the equally bullheaded advocates of states rights at all costs. In the story, on October 9 nine blacks from Cline's farm come to the Paxmores'. Bartley openly takes them north as his property. All but one, who prefers to go on his own, cross the border safely. Then Rachel Paxmore and her brother take over, leading the fugitives to the Hicks farm near Kennett Square (a name and location dredged up from Michener's memory of an English professor at Swarthmore who lived in an eighteenth-century house between Kennett Square and Avondale). In Philadelphia Rachel Paxmore almost runs into Lafe Turlock and Herman Cline, who are pursuing the slaves. By a campaign of handbills about these notorious slavers, the Quakers force their withdrawal, and the fugitives reach Canada in safety. But there is always heated controversy about those who help slaves to escape. Elizabeth Paxmore deflates those who take refuge in scripture by quoting Deuteronomy 23:13: "Thou shalt not deliver unto his master the servant which is escaped from his master unto thee."

When the Civil War breaks out, Maryland remains in the Union. Colonel Janney, who is serving with Jeb Stuart, "the Prince Rupert of the day," comes to recruit for the South. Sixty-seven men, a fourth of them Turlocks, enlist at Patamoke (although only two of them actually own slaves). Nineteen of these men die, including Major Mark Steed, who is killed at Gettysburg. In 1863 blacks are recruited for the Union army at Patamoke, among them the two Cudjo sons and some two hundred of the Steed slaves. In later years the whites from that area who served in the Union army say that they fought for the South. Who would want to fight alongside niggers?

It is a relief to the reader to get away from the slavery question, and the particularly ponderous statements by which Paul Steed supports that institution. In "Voyage Eleven: 1886" and "The Watermen" we get a delightful genre study of life on Chesapeake Bay. Indeed, "The Watermen" was published separately in 1979 as a record of a special way of life. Overall, in a golden age from 1890 to 1920 the Eastern Shore was allowed to sleep undisturbed in its "somnolent estuaries and secluded coves." Undisturbed except for the great hurricane of 1886 (much like the one in 1972), which caused such floods that the Susquehanna deposited more silt in the Chesapeake in four days than it normally did in sixty years. This was an ecological disaster, for once not man-made, for the diminution of salt in the water caused oysters to perish. The fishing industry was prostrated for years.

It is that industry, along with game hunting, that is the center of life in the region. At this point in the novel, those chiefly engaged are the Turlocks, the Camenys (recent Irish immigrants), and the Caters. In 1897 Big Jimbo Cater buys a Turlock boat, which he renames the *Eden*, and one of the Turlocks is even willing to serve under him. It is a brutal life—warding off attacks from Virginia interlopers, shanghaiing boatmen from bars in Baltimore and then cheating them of their wages, battling storms in the often tempestuous bay. It is a brutal life also in the wholesale killing of geese by multibarreled guns. We have in this section a renewal of the epic qualities of life in the earlier days of the region, along with a distinctive set of folkways, values, and conceptions of manhood. There are fine vignettes of shooting expeditions, recipes for oyster stew—in short, a window open onto a distinctive way of life.

There is one more episode in the struggle for Negro freedom. The Steeds and other plantation owners sponsor an amendment to the Maryland constitution that will deny the vote to Negroes. The Turlock clan, predictably, is "savagely supportive," as stereotype continues to outweigh personal experience. Emily Paxmore, a teacher, rushes to the defense of the defenseless and defeats the amendment by tactics that she feels are more Jesuitical than Quaker. She and her followers never mention that Negroes are the target of the amendment. Instead they point out how all European immigrants after a certain date will be disenfranchised. The citizens of the urban centers defeat the bill, though the Eastern Shore votes for it.

As was the case with *Centennial*, the last two sections of this novel attempt to do too much. The region is changing. There is emerging a sense of identity among blacks and the determination to fight for that identity. Patamoke, where over one fourth of the population is Negro, remains "a closed little world" in 1938. Lawton Steed's *A True History of Patamoke* manages to record three hundred years of history without mentioning the blacks. As the narrator says,

In obedience to the national custom, the black experience was erased, not because it was unimportant, but because in the mind of a man like Lawton Steed it never existed.

The novel provides a telling description of the "diminished" state of Negro life. When the Chesapeake Bay bridge is built, white workmen are imported from the North. Educational resources for blacks are minimal; there is discrimination in hospitals on the personal, if not on the medical, level. The Caters of the new generation become activists against segregation. During a riot a residential area burns and sparks ignite the Paxmore boatyard—another irony of history, for it has been the Paxmores who have led the fight for the blacks for more than two centuries.

On the whole, the Steed and Paxmore lines are in a quiescent state. The vigorous Turlock strain, however, has been further enriched by crossing with the Irish Camenys and the German Pflaums, who are the backbone of the river towns. At the end of the 1950s the Eastern Shore is deserted by Oren Steed, Lawrenceville and Princeton, who goes into the oil business in Tulsa, and by Pusey Paxmore, Harvard Law School, who becomes "the conscience of the White House." As the novel ends, these sons come home. Oren buys a two-hundred-acre estate in the marsh area. During the cold winter of 1976 he and his wife quickly identify with the past. They struggle mightily to succor starving birds, even borrowing a navy helicopter to scatter feed on the icy shore. They are almost one with this "wilderness of beauty." Pusey, who has served his term in prison for involvement in Watergate, withdraws from social intercourse almost entirely (except as commodore of the time-honored skipjack race in October 1977). He goes over the disaster of his life again and again in thought and finally in conversation with Oren Steed. He concludes that as far as he was concerned it was "a failure of moral intelligence," and commits suicide that November.

"Voyage Fourteen: 1978" is unaccompanied by a narrative. It records Pusey Paxmore's funeral and the hurricane that batters Peace Cliff that night.

Incessant waves which eleven thousand years ago had delivered detritus to this spot, causing an island to be born, had come back to retrieve their loan

—which would be used and reused

until that predictable day when the great world-ocean would sweep in to reclaim this entire peninsula, where for a few centuries life had been so pleasant.

Against this timeless ebb and flow man's petty pace seems of little importance. The rot of the great world has reached Patamoke through Pusey Paxmore's deficient moral understanding. The Turlocks by their venture into real estate development will no doubt for a time upset the ecological balance of the Eastern Shore. There will be at least a blazing summer as vengeful Caters fling their anti-segregation brands. But all this shall pass into the promised Ozymandian landscape of the ever-changing sea. Meanwhile what the reader has savored through Michener's loving re-creation is a special backwater world which has been and is part of the great American experiment.

The Covenant

Of Michener's major works this one, of 1980, has had the least favorable reception, both in South Africa, where that was to be expected, and in this country, where indifference or a desire to ignore troubled conscience may be the reason. It is true that in *The Covenant* Michener failed to maintain a delicate equilibrium of historical fact and fictional illumination. Also, the episodes are less distinct and therefore less memorable or less dramatically indicative of the course of history in South Africa. But whatever the falling-off in this work, it still must command attention, for it is a massive indictment of racism, self-regarding religious bigotry, and in general arrant, not to mention arrogant, parochialism. The immediate target is South Africa, but the problems there exhibited are endemic to mankind.

Though the narrative seems to touch base in historical data for almost every calendar year during nearly three centuries, it is, like its predecessors, broken up into numbered chapters or episodes. Each of these is headed by a wood-block image of an African animal. These are not symbolic, but they are suggestive of a "nature red in tooth and claw" motif that runs throughout the book, for its action is a fine example of survival of the fittest, in a strictly limited sense. There are two maps as endpapers, one of contemporary southern Africa, the other showing the "Travels and Treks" of the fictional characters. The book also provides three genealogical charts, one of the Van Doorns, who came to the Cape of Good Hope in mid-seventeenth century and who dominate the novel; a second of the Saltwoods, English landed gentry, two of whom go to South Africa early in the nineteenth century; and a third of the Nxumalo, from a black tribe, whose ancestry is extrapolated backward to about 1450 but whose presence in the novel proper begins at the end of the eighteenth century. The cast is large. It would have been easier on the reader if more families, and less closely related families, had been used, though, of course, part of the point of the social indictment is that the society portrayed is clannish and inbred, isolating itself from the rest of the world.

The opening episode, properly entitled "Prologue," introduces the reader to a Bushman named Gumsto, the four-foot-ten-inch head of a clan of twenty-five members. Impelled by drought, the clan is wandering southwest, pursuing a rhino in the hope of a last big meal before going into the desert. Gumsto's son Gao is not, in his father's opinion, developing the way he should to become a leader. When the older man is wounded and Gao takes over, he paints furiously on the rock walls. His work, however, goes beyond literal rendition and opens his father's eyes to the nature of man. The old man is left behind to die, as is the necessary custom, but he is content, for his son has shown him a higher truth.

"Zimbabwe," the second section, is also in the nature of a prologue, establishing as fact what South African prejudice, even on the part of Cecil Rhodes, feels bound to deny. To the European mind, "circumscribed by fear and ignorance, those handmaidens of despair," African history began after the fall of Constantinople in 1453. It was the circumnavigation of Africa after that date that fixed the continent in the Renaissance mind. There it fused with the Biblical notation of gold from the mines of Ophir, which has been identified as the city of Zimbabwe, the high point of black culture in Africa. We see a young man named Nxumalo decide to leave the confined existence of his tribe and go north, reaching the Limpopo River on the seventeenth day and eventually arriving at Zimbabwe, "a thoroughly organized, thriving community with a brilliant business capacity." The ruler of the city notices Nxumalo, who in time becomes inspector of mine production (mines where Bushmen are imprisoned for life—a short life). He is sent on a trading expedition that takes him to an Indian Ocean port and by Arab dhow for 1,100 miles farther. When he returns to Zimbabwe at the end of 1459, he learns that the king has decided to abandon the city because of grave ecological imbalance. The king, says the narrative voice, is a real ruler; the shaman (or high priest) knows how to banish fear and control passions; Nxumalo, though from limited beginnings, has a pragmatic mind and is capable of growth. Any of the three could have learned to function in any society then existing. "These three might be called savages, but they should never be called uncivilized."

With this historically misty beginning out of the way, the novel comes to the European settlement of South Africa, a casual by-product of Dutch domination of the East Indies. The Cape of Good Hope area was unclaimed until 1652, though it was an occasional provisioning station for ships of Portuguese, Dutch, and

British nationality. In 1637 a Captain Nicholas Saltwood of Plymouth, England, arrives on the ship *Acorn* with ten convicts who, as an alternative to hanging, are to be put ashore to start a colony. On May 23 all the convicts drown while attempting to land. When a young Hottentot appears, he is taken on as a sailor and called Jack, the closest the English sailors can come to the clicking sound of Hottentot speech. In Java he becomes friends with a young Dutch boy, Willem van Doorn. Some years later, after the fall of the Portuguese stronghold at Malacca, Willem and his brother Karel are on their way to Holland to establish themselves in the world when their ship is driven aground at the Cape. To protect their precious cargo they build a fort, and Willem remains with the contingent that is to guard it. Hottentots appear, Jack among them. Willem is receptive to his suggestion that his tribe be allowed to come and live at the fort. The Dutch officers will have nothing to do with such an idea. The first chance of racial amity and cooperation is missed.

The great family Bible that Willem rescues from the ship is placed in a dry cave. As he dips into it, he is thrilled by the solemn promise: "And I will establish a covenant between me and thee." Clearly the Dutch have been chosen for this new land. But the officers of the East Indies Company in Amsterdam do not share that enthusiasm. The settlement at the Cape is merely a mercantile operation; no permanent colony is envisaged. However, in 1657 Willem and others are allowed to move to farms beyond Table Mountain. These nine men are the first free white men in South Africa and the progenitors of whatever nation will come to exist. But they are hemmed in by the kinds of moral and social restriction that will produce the rigid self-righteousness of the South African nation. Karel van Doorn, now a haughty official in Amsterdam, turns down a new Hottentot proposal of cooperation. When captured slaves are introduced into the colony from all over the eastern world, harsh repressive laws are set up to keep them from running away. A hedge of bitter almond in fact separates the tiny colony physically from the rest of Africa. Willem himself is punished for his sympathy for the non-white elements and his resistance to bureaucratic restriction. Looking "down the long corridor of Cape history... [he] saw with tragic clarity the total disappearance of Jack and his Hottentots."

Almost a century of expansion, of conflict with native tribes, and of increasing rigidity of moral outlook among the Dutch settlers is conveyed in the fifth chapter, "The Trekboers," so named after the farmers who keep moving outward from the Cape, "tiptoeing through paradise," as they call it. Restless people like Hendrik van Doorn keep pushing east as the soil is depleted. Inevitably they encounter blacks of the Xhosa tribe, who are pushing westward. In their first meeting caution rather than hostility is the norm.

An interesting encounter of another sort is that of Hendrik's son, Adriaan van Doorn, and his wife with Dr. Nels Linnart, nephew of the Swedish naturalist Linnaeus. Though he revels in the new world and the species of plants it affords, Linnart is a critical observer when it comes to social institutions. His report on this outpost of Europe is by no means favorable. In Cape Town, a miserable community of fewer than 3,000 inhabitants, "the avaricious Compagnie" provides no amenities for the common people, though its representatives live luxuriously. A comparison with the British colonies in North America underlines the deficiencies of the Cape. There are no printing presses, no lively newspapers, no colleges, no men like Dr. Franklin. In additon, Linnart, expecting to speak French, discovers that there is no one to talk to. "Custom and the measures of Compagnie rule have eradicated the language," even among the Huguenot émigrés from France and Belgium.

Out of the casual, almost happy-go-lucky frontier living of the Hendrik van Doorns emerges their grandson, Lodevicus, who becomes a gigantic patriarchal figure and who is gigantic also in the explosive rigidity of his vision. At his grandfather's funeral he asks to be baptized. A few years later he has a mystic vision in which God characterizes him as "the hammer who shall slay the infidel." As a young man he journeys to the Cape in order to learn to read and marries Rebecca, a minister's daughter. The young couple have the illuminating thought that the Trekboers are the new Israelites, that they must now settle down and build houses of stone, establishing a permanent moral and social discipline. The two are hard toward Dikkop, the grandfather's old companion, for he is of the tribe of Ham, who are condemned to be slaves forever. Lodevicus traps and slays ninety Bushmen. He and his wife force the parents to leave. When the parents return to the newly built stone house at De Kraal—meaning "the protected place"—Adriaan feels himself imprisoned. His wife tells him that the big prison is, in effect, the ideas that Lodevicus wants to enforce. There is no place for people like Adriaan in this new world. Lodevicus is the inexorable force of the future, the "hard-grained, just human being who was needed at that moment in history."

In 1778 the Dutch authorities, seeking an end to border conflict, decree that whites and natives shall be permanently separated, each group to stay in their present location. Adriaan defies this order and goes into Xhosa territory, where he and his wife are killed by the blacks. Lodevicus, taking terrible revenge, violates and destroys the truce. The Xhosa plan vengeful extermination of the whites, opening a period of continual warfare with uncertain outcome.

During the Napoleonic Wars the Cape region passes back and forth between English and Dutch ownership. The South Africans find that Dutch indifference is equaled by English imperiousness. They want to be left alone, but they have no conception of their inadequacies. Seventy-five percent of the people living in South Africa are unable to read; the Dutch merchant mind has completely stifled the scientific, the creative, the political urges of the inhabitants. The novel asserts: "In South Africa the Old Testament triumphed over the university because it was the university," and states that few nations were ever so solidly indoctrinated in one set of principles. But Lodevicus's battle cry that "South Africa is Dutch and will always remain so" rests on deliberate misrepresentation, for only forty percent are of Dutch ancestry. The rest are of German and Huguenot extraction, with a five-percent admixture of Malay, Hottentot, and black.

Though sufficiently remote in time to have epic proportions, this formative period is treated not nearly as heroically as similar periods in other Michener novels. To have done so would have been to underline a monstrous paradox: how could human beings of such vitality have gone so wrong? Certainly at the midpoint of the novel we are aware that the worm is irremovably in the apple, that the serpent has insinuated himself into Eden, that the descent to Avernus will be appallingly easy.

The second portion of this novel continues such an alternation of the heroic and the stubbornly malefic, under English rule, until South Africa casts herself off from that rule completely in 1960, denying queen, commonwealth, and English concepts of law in one fell, cumulative swoop. This is the only Michener work in which he deals with English culture in any detail. Nevertheless, there is a kind of mellow, kindly light thrown over the milieu from which his second major family, the Saltwoods, come. The unhurried ease and beauty of

their tradition-surrounded life in Salisbury looking across
the meadow at the soaring English cathedral is a point
of reference for the reader as well as for these fictional
Saltwoods of South Africa.

When the master of *Acorn*, whom we met early in
the novel, became rich from his voyage to the Indies,
he had settled in Salisbury; his descendants became landed
aristocrats, Joseph Saltwood entering Parliament from
the rotten borough of Old Sarum. Saltwood has four
sons to place in the world. One of them disappears into
the wilds of North America and is not heard of again
(though one of his descendants does turn up in South
Africa). The eldest, Peter, takes his father's place in Salisbury. Richard, an army officer, goes off to India and
is later sent to South Africa. It is Hilary, the second son,
who becomes a missionary, not a proper clergyman,
joining the London Missionary Society sponsored by
dissident protestants. For these clergymen there is no
predestination. All men can be saved. It is their task to
bring the message of Christ to savages living in darkness.
No sooner does Hilary land at Table Bay in 1810 than
he is accosted and accused of spreading heretical lies, for
his mentor, Reverend Kerr, when he was in South Africa
had stood up for the Hottentots and the Xhosa.

What the novel provides in the section entitled "The
Missionary" is a stark conflict and contrast between the
evangelical and somewhat wooly-headed Hilary Saltwood and the adamantine Lodevicus van Doorn, who
"like all the Van Doorns [is] obsessed with freedom, but
only for himself." Hilary takes Emma, a native girl, as
his consort and has the humiliation of being jilted by an
English girl sent out to him. Her pleasurable intercourse
on board ship with Thomas Carleton makes her prefer
him. Hilary is reviled and despised on all sides. He does
marry Emma (in the sight of God, at least), and they
move to the northeast, where no white man has ever
penetrated before. Later, a trip home is a social ordeal,

though Hilary's mother rises to the occasion and accepts
Emma. Reverend Kerr, Sir Peter Saltwood, and Hilary
argue over how to end slavery. Hilary is for the individual first; Kerr is for principle. Hilary returns to his
lifetime mission in Africa, only to be murdered along
with his wife at the age of forty-three. Their children
are left in the care of the Hottentots, in time to merge
into nonentity.

A third family line emerges, or re-emerges, in the
boy Nxumalo, who is eleven in 1799, a descendant of
the Nxumalo who went to Zimbabwe nearly four centuries before. When in a witch-doctor-dominated tribe
his father is put to death for being happy, the boy runs
away and joins Shako, another lad, who has been cast
off by his Zulu tribe. The latter rises to power, kills his
enemies, is moved by megalomania, and out of his genius for organization and warfare creates a large, unified
Zulu nation. In October 1827 an orgy of hysterical violence lasts three months. Nxumalo, who has often been
in danger, finally gives up his loyalty to Shako when
the death of his third wife is ordered. Shako is killed.
Nxumalo and his confederates flee. They find a scene
of desolation in the wake of the ravages of another de-
mented leader; probably this man and Shako have been
responsible for more than a million deaths in the period
of a decade. However, Shako has become a noble legend
to support a sense of nationhood, and also a taste for
violence, among the Zulus.

More diffuse but central to the growth of the South
African nation is the section entitled "The Voortrek-
kers," the subject of which is the heroic seven-year-long
migration of the Boers across the Orange River to lands
beyond the reach, they hope, of English law and English
custom. Lodevicus's son Tjaart is the proprietor of the
Van Doorn farm at De Kraal, where the original five
thousand acres have been expanded by an additional
sixteen thousand to which they have no title. When

word is received that slavery will be abolished on December 31, 1834, the Van Doorns and others are so outraged that they decide to give up their flourishing farms and cross the mountains into Natal, where they will form a nation of their own. The Boers draft a statement of grievances in justification of their decision: (1) the government is not capable of defending settlers against invasion; (2) the government has taken slaves from them without adequate and honest compensation; (3) the government has appointed preachers who do not know the Boers' language and teachers who want to erase their mother tongue. They declare that they are leaving without rancor, threats, or ill will "to establish in the north a nation more obedient to God's will." Then Jacoba van Doorn points out the omission of their most important grievance, that they have been asked by the British "to form a society in which the proper distance between master and servant is not respected."

On March 15, 1836, the Van Doorn party cross the Orange River. Their total expedition is made up of nearly two hundred wagons and some fourteen thousand Boers, among whom only two are able to read:

They were an intransigent, opinionated group of Dutchmen whose isolation had caused them to turn their backs to the liberalizing influences of the eighteenth century.

When the leaders of the group meet with a native tribe, Van Doorn heeds a warning and survives. His friend De Groot does not, and all fifty-two of his band are slain, except for his son Paulus, who happens to be with the Van Doorns. Tjaart in retaliation kills one hundred and sixty-seven of the natives without suffering any casualties. A few months later the Boers are warned that Dingane, a chieftain with whom they are then meeting, plans to kill them. Van Doorn leaves; another leader does not, and he and seventy others plus thirty Coloureds are slain. In still another encounter an entire Van

Doorn family is killed. To Tjaart it is "obvious that God
has struck His chosen people with a series of punishing
blows. For their arrogance and their sins He has chas-
tened them." Tjaart decides to chasten Dingane and his
forces. On the eve of battle he exhorts the Boers: "One
man of you shall chase a thousand: for the Lord your
God, He it is that fighteth for you, as He hath promised
you." In the Battle of Blood River in December 1838,
between three thousand and four thousand Zulus die.
The only wound among the Boers is a cut hand. Jubilant
over their victory, the Boers reach an arrogant and un-
founded conclusion. They offer God a covenant (whereas
it is for God to offer a covenant to His people). In this
reversal of form God is under no obligation. But in the
conviction that He is under obligation the Boer nation
becomes "a theocracy, and would so remain."

When Tjaart learns that the British are coming to
Natal, he decides to go to Transvaal. There surely he
and his people will be undisturbed. In February 1843 the
migrants reach Vrymeer after seven years of wandering.
The eastern shore of the lake is already occupied by
Nxumalo and his family, but the whites and the blacks
share the land in harmony. Tjaart opposes enslavement
of natives, but after a commando raid eleven surviving
children are saved to work for the Van Doorns as serv-
ants—an analogy with the ancient Canaanites.

The Saltwood family are representative of British
civilizing force and British imperialism in the last decades of the nineteenth century. They are a leaven which
the rigid Boers will resist and which in their triumphs
the Boers will look down upon much as they do upon
the Coloureds. Richard Saltwood has to deal with the
results of a native medicine man's order that his people
kill the cattle and let the fields lie bare in preparation for
the dead to rise and help them reclaim lost territories.
Some seventy to eighty thousand people die, as well as
two hundred thousand cattle. Saltwood mobilizes food

for the starving and also handles the settling of German immigrants who arrive in 1857. He next recruits laborers from India, more than two hundred of them; these are the final element in South Africa's "racial crucible," which is already made up of Bushman, Hottentot, Xhosa, Zulu, Afrikaner, Englishman, and Coloured. Saltwood is knighted for his labors but tells his brother in England that he foresees trouble with the Boers.

Frank Saltwood, Sir Richard's grandson, is at Oriel College, Oxford, when he encounters an older and irregular student from South Africa. On the long voyage home he comes to know him well. The man is C. J. Rhodes, who is already a member of the South African Parliament. This man's enthusiastic vision picks up Ruskin's charge to youth to make England again the center of life. Rhodes sees this in terms of making the map all red; that is, of establishing continuous dominion from the Cape to Cairo, for "The world can be saved only by Englishmen standing together." Believing in white superiority, Rhodes sends Frank off to Zimbabwe to get evidence that will quash black claims that they had a great ancient civilization. Frank finds that they did but dares not tell Rhodes.

The Boers are the great obstacle to Rhodes's dreams. "They huddle in their little republic and refuse to join the mainstream of the human race." He professes to love them for their sturdiness, but finds they lack vision. The blacks, of course, should never be allowed to rule. Rhodes decides to destroy the Boer republics in order to unite the country, not to mention the fact that the newly discovered gold at Witwatersrand is in a Boer republic. The opposition of forces is neatly summed up: "Stubborn, opinionated, God-driven" for President Paul Kruger, who is a child of the Great Trek, a man for whom the Bible is the only book he ever read and who believes the world is flat; for Cecil Rhodes the epithets are "Relentless, self-assured, empire-driven." When

Rhodes is dying at the early age of forty-nine, Frank Saltwood tries to comfort him for his failure to unite South Africa by assuring him that the name of Rhodesia assures him of a lasting monument to his achievements—an irony of which a reader in the 1980s is fully aware.

The Boer War (1899–1902) was not only unnecessary but it was carried on incompetently by the British. The Boers had a maximum force of 3,000 men against an eventual British army of 250,000. The Boers, though undisciplined, knew how to live off the country. The British did not. The war should have been over by Christmas, but the British fought by rule and lost battles they should have won. Ineptitude characterized the effort to relieve besieged Ladysmith, which took an incredible ninety-five days. Not only did the British nearly lose the war, they did lose the peace by their scorched-earth policy, by their concentration camps, and by reason of adverse newspaper reports about Boer heroism and British brutality. Paulus de Groot's commando force, undeterred by the end of the war, continued to strike everywhere; 200,000 British troops had to stay on in an effort to capture him. British reprisals were heavy-handed. The novel relates that in one camp three Van Doorns die, though Sybilla manages to save six-year-old Detlev, whose mental and moral orientation are molded by this experience.

After the basically expository account of the war and its aftermath, it is a relief to have in Detlev van Doorn a character of some magnitude, even though we may consider him a moral monster. He dominates the twentieth-century portion of the novel; indeed, he sums up and embodies the moral aims of and political means to apartheid. He is told that he must learn English so that he may turn their own cleverness against them. He is to accept English in his mind but keep Dutch in his heart. He is indoctrinated in racial discrimination, delighting in an image of South Africa as a multicolored glass of jelly, in which the clear jelly at the top is the Afrikaners, the colored jellies representing the lesser breeds. When he goes to the Cape for his education, he experiences the culture gap existing between Transvaal and the more civilized south, between Vrymeer and the university town of Stellenbosch, where some of the professors are so benighted as to view South Africa as "a mixture of cultures striving to achieve a central tendency." There is never any doubt in Detlev's mind as to what the essential central tendency is. He is for a brief moment disturbed by the loveliness of Clara van Doorn of the older branch of the family at Trianon, but when he sees her kissing Timothy Saltwood, he repudiates her as an English-lover and marries Maria Steyn.

Detlev, who Afrikanizes his name to Detleef, expounds and epitomizes the parochial separateness of Afrikaner aspiration. They want to have their language, Afrikaans, accepted as the legal equivalent of Dutch. They look upon the church as one and undivided, though containing various subordinate elements "ordained by God, approved by Jesus, and eminently workable in a plural society." In other words, Jesus Christ loves all men equally but he wants "each race to have its own boundaries and not to trespass on the territory of others." In short, the lower orders of society must accept the limitations imposed by their betters. If they do so accept, as part of God's covenant, they will "be a peculiar treasure."

British power is still sufficient to keep the South Africans more or less in line during World War II, though there is strong sentiment on the part of some of these to ally themselves with the Nazis. It is after the war that the dam breaks and the implacable provincialism and bigotry sweep barriers to apartheid away. Detleef, now fifty-one, accepts an inconspicuous place on the Commission on Racial Affairs. He is conspicuous, however,

when he refuses to accept a decoration when the King
of England is on a royal visit to South Africa. In the
election of 1948 Prime Minister Jan Christiaan Smuts,
who has spent his life trying to keep the country together, loses, and at long last the Boers win the dominant position that they have dreamed of since 1795. The
civil service at all levels becomes "almost totally Afri-
kaner-minded and -managed." Sexual relations between
members of different races are made a crime. Specific
racial groups are relegated to designated areas. There is
a permanent record kept of racial identity to prevent
"crossing." In the older provinces the Coloureds have
the right to vote. This disharmony with divine plan
(they are after all "the children of sin") is erased by
legislative action, but the Supreme Court annuls the act.
It takes three years to get a sufficient majority in Parliament to overturn that decision. Finally, in October
1960 a plebiscite vote cuts all ties with England, and the
Union of South Africa leaves the Commonwealth.

The enveloping nature of the policy of segregation
is demonstrated by a series of fictional vignettes of what
happens to both blacks and Coloureds. There is also
discrimination of a less obvious nature against those of
British background or even British sympathies. Laura
Saltwood tells her family to leave because horrible things
are going to happen. She herself is punished for anti-
government activity by being "banned" for five years;
that is, she is forbidden to forgather with more than one
person at a time. People whose families have lived in
South Africa for a century and a half, who think of that
country as based on English law and English institutions, suddenly find themselves treated as aliens, as par-
iahs. (It is Michener's portrayal of this ambivalent state
that has evoked a particularly poignant response from
those who are living in South Africa in that situation.)
The blacks meet their increasingly repressive condition
both by becoming activists and taking refuge in Moz-

ambique and by mounting a crusade for black education so that they can bore from within. Even some Afrikaners see the blight that is falling on their country. As Marius van Doorn says of his father, Detleef, after his death: "Lucky man, he won't have to watch the consequences of his handiwork." Marius warns that the Afrikaners and their supporters will be in "perpetual laager" on the edge of South Africa, increasingly on the defensive against the hordes of natives who feel they have a right to the land.

The final chapter, "Diamonds," brings commentary and indictment from Philip Saltwood, an American geologist and descendant of that Saltwood who disappeared into North America in the early nineteenth century. He spends a Sunday at Venloo, attends service at the Dutch Reformed Church, and notices an enchanting girl named Sannie, who turns out to be a Van Doorn. They take a trip together to a national park, where the scenery is "magnificent in a great, brutal way." They visit the imposing Vortrekker Monument, an "amazing echo of Great Zimbabwe," a monument at which only a small fragment of the population of South Africa would feel welcome. Philip is astonished that officials of the country are willing to risk the destruction of the nation in order to prolong their own advantage. The answer to this incomprehension is very simple, if unacceptable to outlanders: "God placed us here to do His work. He put us here to serve as a bulwark of Christian civilization. We must stay." Philip characterizes this group of diehards as a "Götterdämmerung commando."

Philip does at last find what as a geologist he has been looking for: a diamond deposit at perhaps a depth of five hundred feet beneath the lake of Vrymeer, where the vortrekking Van Doorns came to rest. He muses over detritus and history:

Detritus, that's the word. The awful accumulation of wrong decisions, improper turns. You scrape away the excrescences of history...and maybe you get down to the bedrock of human society where diamonds lie."

Whatever Philip's optimism, the overall impression the novel gives is that it is too late for amendment. South Africa is doomed. The covenant has been with the devil, though Michener has been careful not to say so.

The impact of this novel is likely to build over the years if events in the world at large do not deflect attention from moral lessons. What is astonishing in a way is that the novel is a kind of luxury statement. Michener estimates that his

"out-of-pocket expense in bringing this manuscript to its final stages—and I mean my expenses only, not those of Random House or anyone else—was $122,000, which explains why a beginning writer could not possibly write a book like this one.

One begins to wonder if even Michener may have to promote a corporate merger in order to produce *Texas*.

5

Fact, Fiction, and Philosophy

Literary critics, almost without exception, have been cool, if not outright condescending, in their reception of Michener's novels. His style is dull and pedestrian, they say, a sort of mumbling voice. In structure the novels are without complexity or challenge, devoid of illumination by symbol, image patterns, irony, or even parallelism and contrast. His characters, lacking in depth, rarely come alive and certainly don't talk right. And his ideas and value system are deplorably middle-class. Some of this condemnation is just plain sour grapes. How can one find either literary or intellectual grace in a man whose books are read by the millions, who writes for *Reader's Digest*, who always heads the best-seller list and is the darling of book clubs? How tolerate a man who plows ahead on his pedestrian literary way, undismayed by sniping from the sidelines? Such snipers rarely ask themselves what invisible virtue sustains such a readership or what moral vision keeps Michener going in spite of critical disfavor. It is time, however grudgingly, that he be seen at least as a Willie Loman, to whom attention must belatedly be paid.

Historical novels we have had in plenty, but before Michener none that have attempted to represent and sum up a historical span of centuries. Benito Pérez Galdós, the Spanish novelist whose *Episodios Nacionales* cover Spanish history from 1805 to about 1880, is the pioneer in this vein. His panorama is made up of forty-six novels of about two hundred pages each. There is no indication that Michener knew Galdós's work. He does credit Balzac with having provided a model of what novels ought to be. But Balzac's chronicle is in no way comprehensive, and is limited to events in French life during a period of less than fifty years. What Michener seems to have done is to take the examples of Balzac, Zola, and Dos Passos and stretch them to panoramic histories covering three or four hundred years, or in the case of *The Source* several thousand years.

The effort at explaining history by way of fiction is laudable, though the product is almost certain to be found imperfect, if it is to be judged by conventional critical standards. The chief casualty is character development. Assuming that at most a couple of hundred pages is all that can be devoted to members of a given generation, it is likely that the characters will be two-dimensional with very little complexity of action, let alone of thought or emotion. They are, by the demands of the novel, more representative than individual. Some, to be sure, do impose themselves on memory and imagination. This may be because they do dominate certain historical episodes and therefore get considerable exposure. Or they may correspond with and verify already existent stereotypes in the reader's mind—one thinks of the Reverend Abner Hale in *Hawaii* as an example of this. And it is also possible that even though they are not fully developed, some characters loom large because even in their monolithic state they expand the reader's experience and are established as exemplars of a hitherto unknown area of experience. Pasquinel in *Centennial* immediately comes to mind, as does Lodevicus van Doorn in *The Covenant*. Both are larger than life; both are motivated by simple passions. They are men of action, not of thought, in situations where action unimpeded by the hesitations of conscience is necessary and therefore good.

Other characters like Nyuk Tsin in *Hawaii*, the Hoopoe Bird in *The Source*, and Jake Turlock in *Chesapeake* are unforgettable because of their unique personalities. Whether or not they sum up the characteristics of a certain time and place, we like to think they do, and they lodge in affectionate remembrance for that reason. With some frequency, less central characters also come off well. They are sufficiently individualized by some special action or situation, even though motive and feeling are not really explored. Pusey Paxmore comes to mind, or Charlotte Buckland, or Rosalind Steed. When one stops to think about it, one finds that Michener's novels are almost as memorably populated as those of Dickens, certainly more so than those of Balzac.

What is technically known as point of view—that is, the position from which the reader is allowed to see the persons and events of a novel—has been perhaps Michener's greatest problem. The difficulty that he encountered has been exacerbated by the size of his novels but is due basically to his own uncertainty. He seems for a long time to have felt that a third person omniscient narrator would undermine the veracity of historical fiction, that the past had to be attested by a first-person voice. He used such an approach in both *Tales of the South Pacific* and *Sayonara*, but not in *The Bridges at Tokori*, so he was reasonably skilled in either approach. In *Hawaii*, resort to an occasional and unidentified first person in what seems otherwise to be a third-person narrative is confusing as well as unnecessary. The handling of both *The Source* and *Centennial* is ingenious, though possibly more trouble than it is worth. Their contemporary frame narrative with known and vocal personalities commenting on the past is intended to validate the third-person presentation of the historical episodes, though for most readers that is hardly necessary. However, since Michener was aiming at a very broad public, he may have felt that he should assure them of such validation. It is only in *Chesapeake* and *The Covenant* and *Space*, that he seems to have concluded that narrative artifice is unnecessary.

The special problem of Michener's historical novels is how to cover several hundred years of history without the reader's feeling that he has been submerged by a flood. The best solution came in *The Source*, where there was no alternative to complete separation of the fifteen historical narratives, since they are many hundreds of years apart. Although Michener claims that the episodes in *Centennial* are equally self-subsistent, that is not accurate. Especially in the later sections unity is fractured by the necessity of keeping other narrative strands up to date. *Chesapeake* is less subject to this criticism, partly because the episodes are fairly widely separated in time. *The Covenant*, covering more than three hundred years, is unfortunately continuous narrative history with insufficient pointing up of individual episodes. The reader rarely gets his head above water.

In magazine interviews Michener is apt to deny that he is a historical novelist. What he is apparently unwilling to be identified with is the swashbuckling romance of cloak and sword, the tale of hectic and superlative exploit with minimal grounding in fact. But the historical novel is not necessarily of extravagant cast. It can be, and in this century most often is, a serious effort to explain what happened in the past either in the hope of resolving uncertainty or out of a desire to instruct by way of the delights of fiction. Such efforts afford a considerable range of products. There may be novels like Jules Romains' *Les Hommes de Bonne Volonté* (*Men of Good Will*) that attempt to render the moral and intellectual spirit of an age with as little attention to historical figures and events as possible. Or there may be the heavily documented, palpably furnished narratives where fact balances, if it does not outweigh, fiction. It is, on the whole, to this latter category that Michener belongs.

Michener divides novelists into two large groups, those like Flaubert, "who patiently invent one character of superlative meaning and build their books about that one," and those like Dickens, "who prodigally see fictional characters every time they step onto the street."[1] Balzac and Tolstoy, in his opinion, belong in this second group, to which he too belongs. He says that his problem normally would be "to eliminate, not invent, for I had lived, and sometimes intimately, with my potential characters." However, he does not usually model his characters after actual persons, since he wants "the character to have more freedom than the man in life had. I want it to be more flexible, but you obviously have to start with some known experience or some known human being."[2] Though he does not always concede it, Michener has said that he is "not very good at plotting; it doesn't interest me at all. I could end my books anywhere and start anywhere. It's of no concern to me. I give a kaleidoscopic view"—certainly not a psychological one in the manner of Proust, Joyce, or Lawrence.

When he came to write *About Centennial*, Michener reflected on his goals and practice with some acuity:

The purpose of a writer like me—and I am a peculiar one not well fitted to serve as a model for others—is to create a universe in which the reader must surrender himself totally for an extended period of time. If he will do so, he will acquire understandings, images and memories which will rest with him for a long time. The creation of this universe requires all the art the writer can command; it is a painstaking task which cannot be done quickly, and every component of the finished book must contribute to the illusion.[3]

He told students at the University of Oregon in 1961,

"I'm didactic and persuasive and hortatory and everything else that a novelist should probably not be. I take my lessons from Balzac and Zola and Dreiser and that group—a very honorable group of preceptors. I do start with conflicts. I do start with something I want to get across. I do start with some social observations that I want to make.[4]

John Kings, who was close to Michener when he was writing *Centennial*, says that the author wants his readers to find enough information in the novels to make them just as viable in twenty-five years' time. "He writes them to last, and he says exactly what he wants to say, irrespective of whether some readers will want to stay with him all the way."[5]

On the whole, the novels live up to these diffuse and at times contradictory descriptions. For some reason Michener will deny that he is in the "blockbuster syndrome," arguing that he has produced a lot of books (nonfiction mostly, as it happens) that do not fit that pattern. Nonetheless, as was stated earlier, it is likely that his reputation will come to rest on *Hawaii* and the big novels that have followed it, on the individual blend of fact and fiction that characterizes his major works.

There can be no doubt that Michener's mature novels are saturated by fact. It is on these terms that the reader must accept or reject them. And it seems to me that it is acceptance of these terms that accounts for the vast readership which Michener has built up over the last quarter of a century. It may be that when readers put down his books three-fourths of the way through, they are saying that they have had enough facts in that particular reconstituted world, though my own feeling is rather that they find Michener's descriptions of recent or contemporary life banal; that is, without illumination beyond what they themselves have already seen. In short, saturation in fact works well for many readers as long as they are curious about the way life *was* at some particular historical period but becomes superfluous, because insufficiently enlivened by style, when it relates to what they already know.

Michener tells us that he always revisits the scene of his novels, never writes from memory. With one exception, this is true in his major works, including *Iberia*. There had been long acquaintance with the landscape, the feel, of Hawaii, of eastern Colorado, and of the Chesapeake Bay area. *The Source* also gives an impression of long-standing familiarity, due perhaps to his general acquaintance with Islamic lands in the Middle East. *The Covenant* does not convey such authenticity. Compare, for example, the desert in *Centennial* with the desert in *The Covenant*. One description produces a felt experience; the other is merely guidebook description.

Beyond the convincing topographical accuracy of most of the novels is an infusion of considerable bodies of factual material which, in all honesty, many readers skip over. This is not necessarily a flaw of magnitude, for materials such as how to make flint arrowheads among the Plains Indians or how ships are built and oyster stew concocted in Chesapeake Bay are certainly relevant to the life depicted. Such bodies of material contribute to the reader's confidence that he is immersed in the real thing. He may on many occasions rejoice that at long last he has got down to the bedrock description of how people really lived. Naturally there will be negative as well as positive reactions. A writer in *Commentary* has complained that Michener's "objective is the factually meticulous transcription of the past in easily comprehensible form, and if he does harbor any pretensions, they are aimed not at the tone and manner of literary artists but at the authority of the historian." In other words, he gives in to people who want to learn without serious intellectual effort.[6]

Factual density and authenticity is a Michener hallmark in the later novels. He and we are stuck with it, and in an age avid for fact it seems to guarantee success. No one has been more meticulous than Michener in attempting to guarantee authenticity. As we have seen, he immerses himself in his material, saying that he can remember "maybe seventy or eighty books that I am working on." But he does not trust his memory. Acknowledgements accompanying each of his books attest to the wide range of experts to whom he submits text or inquiries, often thereby avoiding error, as he tells us in the case of diplodocus, the dinosaur in *Centennial*. Michener originally had him living on land, until his consultant pointed out that the creature was too heavy and had to be an aquatic animal. In the writing of *Hawaii* he depended chiefly on a single expert assistant, with whom he discussed his text in detail. *The Source* was vetted by an antiquarian member of the Israeli Parliament. For *The Covenant* he was particularly dependent on expert opinion, which, he says, was given unstintingly. And, of course, in *Centennial* and *Chesapeake*, since they are both part of our own at least partially known national tradition, we are aware of how many kinds of informed judgment he had available to rely on. But none of Michener's novels is written by anyone else, and they are remarkably free of error so far as fact is concerned.

This solidity of fact does not really compromise Michener's skill as a storyteller. A century ago Henry James said of Zola's novels—which in certain respects are like Michener's—that they were capacious vessels. By analogy, Michener's are supertankers, containing many compartments that are independent parts of the whole. This is especially true of *The Source*, *Centennial*, and *Chesapeake*, where the separation is clear-cut and the individual episodes are for the most part independent narratives. The strategy in these three novels is to illuminate various episodes or periods of history by means of exciting stories. No two writers would select exactly the same kinds of narratives for this purpose. There is bound to be a difference of opinion as to whether the materials chosen do adequately illuminate, but there can be no question that artistic shaping and artistic selection have taken place.

Michener's basis of choice is twofold. He wants simple, ordinary life situations; or where they are not ordinary, he wants them peopled with unglamorous persons. In other words, he wants to avoid distortion by way of the exceptional and the romantic. But he also wants to emphasize the heroic in human endeavor, to show in all five of his major novels the prodigies of valor, of endurance, of unremitting hard work that ordinary people are capable of. In the case of four of the novels the action is the discovery and peopling of new lands. Pioneers of a sort are the chief exhibit. In *The Source* there is physical pioneering in the beginning, but as the centuries go on what we see is incredible endurance against overwhelming odds; in addition, however, there is also a kind of moral pioneering that fuels the stamina that the Jews show. In general terms, a Michener novel is epic in scope and in tone, epic in the assurance, or reassurance, that in days gone by, like the Spear-Danes or the fleeing Trojans or Roland at the Pass of Roncesvalles, ancestors performed deeds of valor.

There can be no doubt that this is the propulsive narrative force that carries readers well into, if not always through, the huge Michener novels. Where will one find a more graphic account of rounding South America by sailing ship? Where a better depiction of the conflict between conquering Roman and puny resistant barbarian? Where the loneliness of the illimitable plains? Where the aggressive sensibility and self-enclosed lives of the denizens of Chesapeake Bay? Only *The Covenant* lacks such engagement for the reader. (The great trek of the Boers, for example, is better rendered in Stuart Cloete's *The Turning Wheels*.) Moreover, there is great variety in Michener's narrative subsections: voyages or journeys of discovery, encounters with native inhabitants, the sheer rigor of a hostile environment, wars on local or national scale, domestic strife, and just plain criminal scheming and aggression. For hundreds of thousands, if not millions, of readers, these narratives lodge in the mind as the basic substance of the national history with which they deal. For better or worse, Michener has illuminated history, has given it body, for more people than any other writer one can name.

The substance of history, factual or fictional or a combination of the two, is only part of the freightage of these novels. By immersion in them the reader is bound to feel the impact of a view of life, a Weltanschauung, that may be overt and is certainly implicit in any representation of past events. Even the historian has to pick and choose from myriad data; he too constructs a past epic, just as the novelist does. What either the novelist or the historian selects helps determine the statement that the work makes. That statement may be simple or complex, fairly impartial or emphatically polemic, traditional or heterodox, but it will be there in the values that it affirms, in the human beings over whose lives it lingers, in the affirmations that the narrative voice or fictional characters utter. Michener makes no bones about the fact that he is a moralist. His critics are equally forthright in their dislike for the values he affirms.

The overriding lesson of the Michener novels (including *Tales of the South Pacific* and *The Bridges at Tokori*) is human courage, a heroic facing up to overwhelming odds. These re-creations of the past make readers feel good about both their ancestors and their own implied capacities. There is the implication that if *they* could do it, so can *we*. There is nothing Pollyannish about this, no bleating optimism. Michener has been careful to point out that, while he does not use sex and violence or sadism as staples of his depictions, his works contain "a tension and an indication that life is a pretty seamy mess. I would never get away from that, because that's how I see it." Like many novelists before him, he does on occasion take evident pleasure in some of his rascals, whose overflow of vitality leads them to hazard strange and slippery paths. But he can never be said to have written a human comedy. His view is much too serious for that. Neither does he offer tragic overtones. Things are as they are—mixed.

At some point the reader is likely to become aware of a philosophical, or perhaps merely tonal, inconsistency. The novels show a past that is heroic, yet in their last episodes—those dealing with recent or contemporary events—they show a present that is confused, divisive, without coherent purpose or system of values. Each of the five historical novels contains a statement, a pious hope at least that, if men and women of goodwill band together and exert the heroic effort characteristic of the past, then a downhill slide can be averted—in the Middle East, in the Great Plains, in rural Maryland and cosmopolitan Washington, D.C., even in a South Africa reeling from the poison of self-ascribed righteousness. Yet such affirmation about the future, it seems to me, is belied by the evidence of disorder and unreason. Only in *Hawaii* is there possibly sufficient evidence for hope. In the other novels it is as though the rousing vision of a heroic past has been summoned up less to give joy and satisfaction in the present than to provide moral armor in a suffering future.

Michener has said of himself that "As writer one looks at the ebb and flow of civilization with a detached eye." That detached eye, he has been saying with some frequency in recent years, sees that the rise and fall of civilizations is a predictable cycle: "Great societies do lose their drive and do go down hill, all of them." He sees the United States as a fragile society, "not as strong inherently as, say Japan," which is unified in race, religion, and social structure. But we are also "a very brilliant society. We have untold capacity, really, for solving any of our problems. We are a very bright, resilient, powerful people." Therefore he thinks that our span of energy may extend to the middle of the twenty-first century. He even held out to Swarthmore students in the fall of 1981 the hope that prudence, good management, and the generation of new ideas could give us another century or two. But he warned also that we could become the Spain and Portugal of this age, going only so far and then letting others take over.

Such exhortation can scarcely be equated with the easy optimism with which some critics charge Michener. Neither, however, is he an absolute doom-sayer. Though he was in college when Oswald Spengler's *The Decline of the West* hit the campuses, he has apparently never subscribed to the Spenglerian doctrine of rigidly programmed culture cycles. Also he avoids the easy and evident parallel between the United States and Rome in transition from republic to empire. He prefers to think that each culture has some flexibility depending on prudence, discipline, and clear-sightedness, although ultimately nothing can stay its fall.

The charge that Maxwell Geismar made in a review of *Hawaii* nearly a quarter of a century ago is ridiculous. He accused Michener of "unthinking acceptance" of modernity and in particular of American modernity, while his deepest feeling and best talent belonged to the past.[7] This was echoed years later by an article in *Commentary* deploring "his urge to reinforce the soggy liberal optimism of his middlebrow audience," not as panderer to it but "because he shares its values and attitudes so completely."[8] I venture to assert that Michener's values and attitudes are more valid and more enduring than those behind the buzz-saw tearing apart of left-wing intellectuals or the reinforced concrete of the troglodytic right. As John Kings has commented, there is a Michener mystique that draws multitudes of readers to him, "perhaps, above all, because he is able as a writer to remind us of the essential values that go to the making of a healthy society."[9]

From the novels we become aware of two values above all others that Michener singles out as important. The first of these is human tolerance, a deliberate diminution of inherited, and possibly inherent, racism. The other is a relation of man to his environment that is healthful and fruitful. These are not necessarily presented in tandem, though in fact they are logically correlative. Man cannot flourish unless he puts the land to proper use. If he exploits it with no view to future needs, then he has diminished productivity, diminished well-being. If there is discrimination against other human beings because of race, color, or place of origin, then there is diminished use of human potential, of human skill, and the result is not merely diminished well-being for those discriminated against but a diminution for the whole society of which they are an insufficiently utilized part.

All of the novels (except *The Bridges at Toko-ri* and *The Drifters*) have discrimination because of race as a major target. This is approached sentimentally and on a limited basis when Nellie Forbush becomes aware of her parochial attitude toward race and succeeds in overcoming it. It is central to *Hawaii*, where the haoles — the American missionaries and their successors — are guilty of a superiority complex that is undermined but not destroyed by the evident virtue of Chinese and Japanese immigrants and is at least challenged by the sybaritic attitudes of the native Polynesians. Another side of the issue is exposed in *The Source*, where the fierce arrogance of the Chosen People is seen to have been the only way they could have survived. Nonetheless, the contemporary framework of that narrative does question whether such arrogance is any longer necessary or tenable and holds out the possibility, however elusive, of a reasonable cooperation between Arab and Jew. *Centennial* and *Chesapeake* face up to the intensity of American racial discrimination, first against Indians, then against imported Negro slaves, and more recently against Mexicans. Neither novel resolves the issue but both assert the dignity and worth of so-called inferior races. Finally, *The Covenant* becomes more tract than novel because of its insistent indictment of South African intransigence, directed not only toward those of dark skin but even against Europeans who do not think as they do. All the novels by their vividness and by the cumulative authority they have given Michener are to a limited extent an inoculation against racism. Their author has to admit, however, that it is not possible to remove prejudice entirely, though it is possible to legislate against discriminatory practices in jobs and schools and government.

The environmental issue is less obvious and less persistent in the Michener novels. As was pointed out, it becomes central toward the end of *Centennial*, which is by far the most devout of the novels in respect to this article of Michener's creed. But the theme is present in *Hawaii* and in *Chesapeake*, where there is a tug-of-war between needed human enterprise to make the land usable and human greed that assumes the fruits need not be shared. In *The Source* and *The Covenant* we find a slightly different emphasis. Both novels show a promised land, flowing with milk and honey, where ease and comfort are perennially destroyed by arrogance. When Michener produces the promised novel on Texas, it will be interesting to see how he handles his two major themes, for to the world outside arrogance appears to be writ large in Texas.

Another value that is consistently present in the novels is the virtue and necessity of hard work. Michener's epic characters are heroic precisely because they

are willing to exert themselves to the full. What Michener admires is drive. What he cannot stand is apathy,
inertia. This raises problems in *The Source*, where for
the most part the Jews who are to survive are counseled
by God to take punishment lying down, to go into exile
unresistingly. This apparent spinelessness is, however,
balanced by the Jews' aggressive belief, by an absolute-
ness of faith and hope in the face of adversity. At the
end of the novel Michener provides more than a suggestion that the time has come for action, not forbear-
ance. In *Hawaii* the native Hawaiians are the chief example
of lack of drive. The Chinese and Japanese, especially
the Japanese on playing field and battlefield, are superb
examples of unfailing will. The pioneer societies of the
other novels abound in such exercise of will, even in the
figures of villains like Skimmerhorn in *Centennial* or
Bonfleur, the pirate, in *Chesapeake*. The most telling
examples of lack of will are the plantation owners in
tidewater Virginia or Maryland, who are content to bask
in the beneficent sun of slavery, by their masterly in-
activity ensuring moral and economic bankruptcy.
Michener makes no bones about his belief in the so-
called Puritan ethic. An energetic seeking of wealth, of
power, of security is certainly preferable to the sin of
sloth. The amendment of too egoistic striving is always
possible by an altruistic expansion of goals. Without
drive as a means there can be no admirable ends. Michener says he feels no guilt over the accumulation of
wealth, and he points out in another connection that in
the United States private support of the arts and of education by those who have made their pile demonstrates
a sense of responsibility far exceeding what is to be found
in other countries.

Part of Michener's wisdom is his acceptance of change
as inevitable, even as a sign of health. He has in the

course of the novels (and *Iberia*) shown a good many rigid societies dying, so to speak, from anemia, forcing their vital youth to break out in one way or another. Institutions—that is, social arrangements for various purposes—are by no means eternal, for they are the product of environmental factors as well as political ones. But though change and progress are not identical throughout the world of bourgeois culture, and in the United States in particular, it is frequently a fundamental article of faith that they are. The human strategy needed in a world of change is to decide upon and take steps to preserve values that are fundamental to human well-being, that maintain or enhance the desired quality of life.

Since Michener believes that the young must at least be listened to, student activism of the late 1960s caused him to bring many of his concerns into focus. The point of a *New York Times Magazine* article entitled "One-and-a-Half Cheers for Change"[10] was that we must accept change, even embrace it, and at the same time control it. The Luddites of the 1960s, who had taken hallowed dissident positions against supersonic planes, apartment houses in the suburbs, chemical fertilizers, and, we may as well add, nuclear power, fluoride in the water, and computers, were on the wrong track by their all-or-nothing attitude, he wrote. A balanced approach was what we needed—neither too much fanaticism nor too much reaction. Women had to be liberated, but not necessarily by the then-current crusade. Black power was desirable, but not black revolution. The aspirations of youth were valid, he asserted, until their protests went beyond "the pattern of what an organized society ought to tolerate." We would henceforth be an urban society. Therefore we should build a number of middle-sized cities from scratch and utilize what we learned from that to save the big cities. In political functioning we had regressed, yes, or at least had lost headway. We must devise new forms to make democracy work. Michener concluded that, having "worked much with the history of older civilizations," he believed that

they fell more because they failed to adjust to change than because they were undermined by it. American democracy had better learn to adjust to change, or it too, will be doomed.

Two short works, *America vs. America: The Revolution in Middle-Class Values* (1969) and *The Quality of Life* (1969–70), took much the same position. Michener accepted youthful ferment as a healthful antidote to middle-class hypocrisy. He charged that TV advertising presented "a portrait of middle-class life which is beneath contempt." He believed that "The old values of demonstrated worth" should be "constantly scrutinized lest they become ritual or cant, carefully weeded from time to time lest they become mere prohibitions." If this were done they should "prove serviceable for generations to come."

The last section of *The Quality of Life* sounded a warning that is the most emphatic Michener has set down in any of his writings, a warning of the potential for disaster in a constantly accelerating overpopulation. It was, he said, "like a cancer, multiplying fantastically and eating up all available sustenance to no constructive purpose. If allowed to proceed unchecked it has got to produce catastrophe." Not only must the United States keep its own population under control, it must watch carefully "the runaway populations of the rest of the world" and adjust to the consequences. Michener was especially concerned, apprehensive really, about population increasees in Mexico and the rest of Latin America. He pointed out further that constantly increasing population aggravated the various problems that he had discussed in this volume and elsewhere.

Every act of national policy must contribute to stabilization of population, and if racial attitudes, religious customs or personal preferences have to be modified, we must modify them.

This is the strongest language Michener has used concerning any social problem. It certainly counters the charge of sentimental optimism that has been leveled against him.

It is difficult to determine to what extent Quakerism has shaped Michener's thought and values. He became a member of the Society of Friends while he was in college and was long listed as an absentee member of the Swarthmore Meeting. He later joined the Bucks County Meeting, in which his absenteeism has been of even longer duration. In spite of his lack of participation in formal religious exercises, Quakerism is clearly important to him, both because it gives him a sense of continuity with a valiant tradition and because it nurtures independence of mind and spirit. Like the Quakers he offers no apology for "getting ahead," but spends little on himself. Like the Quakers he has "a boundless curiosity about life," which to him is also an "essential ingredient for a successful writer." Like the Quakers he tries to avoid identifying conventional moral and social patterns with "basic morality." The result is that he has no hesitation about taking an unpopular position—on race relations, on changing sexual mores, on professional athletics, or even on the legitimacy of rock music as art. Michener does not talk about the Inner Light of conscience that for the Quaker takes the place of verbally sharpened creeds. In general, he feels that churches are more to be valued for their social leavening and social betterment than as debating societies over doctrine. In *Chesapeake* his depiction of the Paxmore family is both admiring and accurate without being sentimental. Quakers have human limitations like other people, but they have a canny knack for doing good in the world.

Unflinchingly aware as he is of social problems, ready as he may be to cut the Gordian knot when there is no other solution, Michener is also deeply stirred by the privileged status of being an American. And no contemporary writer is better situated to measure that privilege. Himself brought up in abject poverty and having been a witness to such poverty all over Asia, he has every reason to rejoice over the time and place in which he has lived for nearly eighty years. As he himself asks, where else could a youth of his origins have escaped poverty and received a superior education? Where else is there such widespread upward social mobility? Where else such cultural diversity? Where else such relative freedom from social and political constraints? Where else such generosity in response to suffering throughout the world? An awareness of American good fortune, and an awareness of the ephemeral nature of all such good fortune, pervade and inform everything that Michener has written for forty years. He is patriotic. He is aware of the sublime duty of citizens to preserve and defend their heritage, and he is angry at the ignorance of those who delight in rending the delicate fabric that holds a society together. But he is by no means uncritical of that society. We must understand the shortcomings as well as the strengths of that society if we are to be effective in preserving it. Complacency, be it of the country club or the pizza parlor, is the last thing we can afford.

The panoramic evocations of history which are Michener's major achievement do not merely celebrate what has been. They are an object lesson in what will forever be needed in the way of vigilance, self-abnegation, and devotion to something larger than oneself. As novelist and essayist Michener seeks to do more than provide fragments to shore against the ruins of a crumbling society—even though all societies crumble eventually. He seeks to bring understanding and renewed zeal to a not-so-muddled majority, made up of us who are middle-class, middle-brow Middle America.

Notes

1. A Traveler in Realms of Gold

1. This system was initiated by Frank Aydelotte, president of Swarthmore for nearly twenty years and American Secretary of the Rhodes Trust.
2. In fact, Robert E. Spiller, one of the leading scholars in the field of American literary history, was teaching at Swarthmore from 1921 to 1945.
3. Orville Prescott, *In My Opinion* (New York: Bobbs-Merrill, 1952), p. 154. In his "Outstanding Novel" column in *Yale Review* 36 (Spring, 1947), 576, he had said of Michener, "He is certainly one of the ablest and one of the most original writers to appear on the American literary scene in a long time."
4. Joe Jares, "The Wrong Man Behind the Mike," *Sports Illustrated* 52 (May 12, 1980), 45.

2. Island Worlds of the Pacific

1. "Reflections of a Nesomaniac," *Reader's Digest* 112 (June, 1978), 189–96ff.
2. John P. Hayes, *Conversations with Writers II* (Detroit: Gale Research Company, 1978), p. 147.
3. James W. Foster, Jr., "Preface," in Howard A. Link, *Primitive Ukiyo-e: From the James A. Michener Collection in the Honolulu Academy of Arts* (Honolulu: University Press of Hawaii, 1980), xvi.
4. See Michener's "Introduction" to Michi Weglyn, *Years of Infamy: The Untold Story of America's Concentration Camps* (New York: Morrow, 1976), pp. 27–31.

5.   "Hawaii: The Case for Our 50th State," *Reader's Digest* 73 (December 1958), 158–72.

4.   NEW LIFE IN NEW LANDS

1.   "Is America Burning?" *New York Times Magazine*, July 1, 1973, pp. 10ff.
2.   John Kings, *In Search of Centennial: A Journey with James A. Michener* (New York: Random House, 1978), p. 56.
3.   *Ibid.*, p. 109.
4.   John Kings designed the Crown V brand of the fictional Venneford Ranch and actually registered it in Wyoming in Michener's name. *Ibid.*, p. 133.
5.   See *ibid.*, Chapter 5, "The Film," for a detailed account of the making of this movie.

5.   FACT, FICTION, AND PHILOSOPHY

1.   *About Centennial: Some Notes on the Novel* (New York: Random House, 1974), pp. 51–52.
2.   John P. Hayes, "James A. Michener," in *Conversations with Writers II* (Detroit: Gale Research Company, 1978) p. 156.
3.   *About Centennial*, p. 49.
4.   "A Discussion with James Michener," *Northwest Review* IV (Spring, 1961), 16.
5.   John Kings, *In Search of Centennial: A Journey with James A. Michener* (New York: Random House, 1978), p. 109.
6.   Pearl K. Bell, 'James Michener's Docudramas," *Commentary* 71 (April, 1981), 72.
7.   Maxwell Geismar, "Gods, Missionaries and the Golden Men," *New York Times Book Review*, November 22, 1959, pp. 4–5.
8.   Bell, *op. cit.*, p. 73.
9.   Kings, *op. cit.*, p. 15.
10. "One-and-a-Half Cheers for Change," *Reader's Digest* 99 (December, 1971), 209–16.

Bibliography

BOOKS BY JAMES A. MICHENER

Tales of the South Pacific. New York: Macmillan, 1947.

The Fires of Spring. New York: Random House, 1949.

Return to Paradise. New York: Random House, 1951.

The Voice of Asia. New York: Random House, 1951.

The Bridges at Toko-ri. New York: Random House, 1953.

Sayonara. New York: Random House, 1954.

The Floating World. New York: Random House, 1955.

The Bridge at Andau. New York: Random House, 1957.

Selected Writings, with a special foreword by the author. New York: Modern Library, 1957.

Rascals in Paradise (with A. Grove Day). New York: Random House, 1957.

The Hokusai Sketchbooks: Selections from the Manga. Rutland, Vt.: C. E. Tuttle Co., 1958.

Japanese Prints: From the Early Masters to the Modern. Rutland, Vt.: C. E. Tuttle Co., 1959.

Hawaii. New York: Random House, 1959.

Report of the County Chairman. New York: Random House, 1961.

The Modern Japanese Print. Rutland, Vt.: C. E. Tuttle Co., 1962.

Caravans. New York: Random House, 1963.

The Source. New York: Random House, 1965.

Iberia: Spanish Travels and Reflections. New York: Random House, 1968.

America vs. America: The Revolution in Middle-Class Values. New York: New American Library, 1969.

Presidential Lottery: The Restless Gamble in Our Electoral System.

New York: Random House, 1969.

The Quality of Life. Philadelphia: Girard Bank, 1970 (with reproductions of paintings by James B. Wyeth); Lippincott, 1970 (revised and without illustrations).

Kent State: What Happened and Why. New York: Random House, 1971.

The Drifters. New York: Random House, 1971.

A Michener Miscellany, 1950–1970 (edited by Ben Hibbs). New York: Random House, 1973.

Centennial. New York: Random House, 1974.

About Centennial: Some Notes on the Novel. New York: Random House, 1974.

Sports in America. New York: Random House, 1976.

Chesapeake. New York: Random House, 1978.

The Watermen: Selections from Chesapeake, New York: Random House, 1979.

The Covenant, New York: Random House, 1980.

James A. Michener's U.S.A.: The Land and the People (edited by Peter Caitlin). New York: Crown Publishers, 1981.

Space. New York: Random House, 1982.

BOOKS AND ARTICLES ABOUT JAMES A. MICHENER

Bell, Pearl K. "James Michener's Docudramas." *Commentary* 71 (April, 1981), 71–73.

Day, A. Grove. *James A. Michener.* Boston: Twayne, 1962; second edition, 1977.

Freed, Eleanor. "A Windfall for Texas." *Art in America* 57 (November, 1969), 78–85.

Hayes, John P. "James A. Michener" in *Conversations with Writers II.* Detroit: Gale Research Company, 1978, pp. 143–80.

Inouye, Hon. Daniel K. "James A. Michener." *Congressional Record,* September 17, 1962.

Kings, John. *In Search of Centennial: A Journey with James A. Michener.* New York: Random House, 1978.

Link, Howard A. *Primitive Ukiyo-e: From the Michener Collection in the Honolulu Academy of Arts.* Honolulu: University Press of Hawaii, 1980.

Mitgang, Herbert. "Why Michener Never Misses." *Saturday Review*, Vol. 7 (November, 1980), 21–24.

Texas University Art Museum. *The James A. Michener Collection*. Austin: University of Texas, 1977.

Index

Selected list of titles (continued from page ii)

Complete list of titles in the series available from publisher on request.

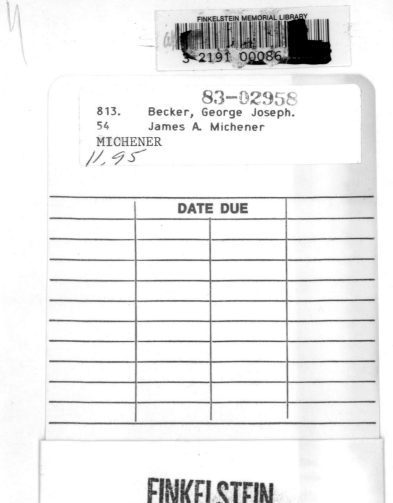